William Gilbert Anderson

Methods of teaching Gymnastics

William Gilbert Anderson

Methods of teaching Gymnastics

ISBN/EAN: 9783337166458

Printed in Europe, USA, Canada, Australia, Japan

Cover: Foto ©Paul-Georg Meister /pixelio.de

More available books at **www.hansebooks.com**

METHODS

OF

TEACHING GYMNASTICS

BY

WILLIAM GILBERT ANDERSON, M.D.,

Associate Director of the Yale University Gymnasium, President of the Anderson Normal School of Gymnastics, Dean of the Chautauqua School of Physical Education, etc.

MEADVILLE, PENN'A
FLOOD AND VINCENT
The Chautauqua-Century Press
M DCCC XCVI

THIS BOOK IS DEDICATED TO MY FATHER,
Edward Anderson,
WHO, TWENTY-FIVE YEARS AGO,
STARTED ME IN THIS WORK,
AND WHO HAS ALWAYS
BEEN MY COUNCILOR
AND ENTHUSIASTIC
SUPPORTER.

CONTENTS.

CHAPTER.		PAGE.
	Introduction	7
I.	Opinions of Educators on Education	16
II.	Opinions of Educators on Physical Education	29
III.	The Ethical Element in Physical Training	40
IV.	The Gymnastic Day's Order	57
V.	Effect of Certain Exercises upon the Pulse-rate	68
VI.	Stimulus, or How to Arouse Interest	76
VII.	Attention	84
VIII.	Discipline, or School Government	95
IX.	Analysis.—Synthesis.—Reflex Acts	111
X.	Why do we Teach?—Who Shall Teach?	115
XI.	Outline Lessons on Parts of the Body	122
XII.	How to Teach Walking	151
XIII.	The Alphabet	158
XIV.	The Voice.—Commands	164
XV.	Hints on Teaching a Class of Boys	171
XVI.	Military Gymnastics	183
XVII.	Use of Light Apparatus	216
XVIII.	Mannerisms	242
XIX.	Division of Work for the Month and Day	245

ILLUSTRATIONS.

		Page
Fig. 1.	Normal Pulse, Standing	73
Fig. 2.	Pulse-rate after Running in Place	73
Fig. 3.	Pulse-rate after Slow Leg Work and Breathing Exercises	73
Fig. 4.	Pulse-rate, in Place Rest	73
Fig. 5.	Turn Head, Wand Front, Stepping	124
Fig. 6.	Letter Y	124
Fig. 7.	The Chest Machine	140
Fig. 8.	Attention	148
Fig. 9.	Knee Bending	148
Fig. 10.	Stepping Motion, Neck Firm	156
Fig. 11.	The Charging Motion	156
Fig. 12.	Foot Placing, Two Foot Lengths	157
Fig. 13.	The Reverse Charge	157
Fig. 14.	Foot Placing, One Foot Length	188
Fig. 15.	Right Arm Out, Left Arm Front, Face to Left, Reverse Charge, Left Leg Front	188
Fig. 16.	In Place Rest	189
Fig. 17.	Measuring Facing Distance	189
Fig. 18.	Form Fours from Twos	208
Fig. 19.	Form Twos from a File	209
Fig. 20.	Form Twos from Fours	210
Fig. 21.	Right, Forward, Fours Right	212
Fig. 22.	Carrying Wand Incorrectly	228
Fig. 23.	Method of Grasping Wand	228
Fig. 24.	Wand Down	229
Fig. 25.	The Single Pendulum	229
Fig. 26.	The Grasp	236
Fig. 27.	The Starting Position	236
Fig. 28.	Start for the Second Circle	237
Fig. 29.	Finish of the Second Circle	237
Fig. 30.	Start for the Half Snake	252
Fig. 31.	Knees Bent for Fencing	253
Fig. 32.	Hips Firm	253
Fig. 33.	Neck Firm	253

METHODS OF TEACHING GYMNASTICS.

INTRODUCTION.

IF an excuse were made for writing this book, it would be that many teachers of gymnastics need it. It cannot be said that the book will contain many new or startling axioms, but it will try to prove that the laws of pedagogy are as applicable to teaching gymnastics as to teaching the three R's. In short, the principles of schooling should be known to instructors in any branch. A teacher may or may not be successful. She may have a fund of knowledge at her disposal; her record in the normal school from which she graduated may have been the best, yet she may fail as an instructor; she cannot impart her knowledge to others. What is it that makes one a good instructor, while another, who has had the same training and stood equally well, fails? This question will be discussed in the following pages. An attempt will be made to lay down teaching rules for the one who trains the body. Experience is a good educator; a wise man learns from the experience of others. Consequently, if one who has made many mistakes during ten years of tuition makes statements based upon his experience, they should be of some value to the beginner.

It will be said that successful teaching is a matter of natural aptitude, or that the instructor possesses a special form of genius. This is only partly true. A person who is greatly interested in a subject, and at the same time anxious to instruct others, can learn to teach. If we were to enforce the law that only those who were born teachers should instruct classes, a large per cent of those who are now giving instruction in this country would drop from the ranks. There are hundreds of born or natural teachers who never give instruction. It would be impossible to find them, and so long as it is necessary for people who are not classified under the head of naturalists to educate, it is well for them to be guided by the laws of pedagogy.

It is time for our teachers to read the various works upon the art of teaching. The theory of gymnastics is fascinating, the practice more so; but the application of the many rules which are found in works on pedagogy has not yet been considered by the majority of physical directors.

The object of this work is not to set forth the claims of or criticise any system but to present methods. One who has not taught teachers will be surprised at the limited knowledge of many of them. Men and women who have been teaching for years violate so many rules of what, in the generally accepted term, is called pedagogy that we are surprised. The fact that these teachers keep their positions, draw fair salaries, and give satisfaction shows that this part of the subject is new not only to the instructor but to the employer.

Experience proves that the laws of pedagogy should be applied to teaching gymnastics, and while the author of this work hesitates to rush into print, he believes it imperative that the teacher should read more and accept the advice of others; he therefore takes the initiative. Teachers read but do not think that they are the ones who will be benefited by the advice. They do not understand a very important rule, namely, *The pupil must be put in a teachable condition.* It makes no difference what the age, the rule holds good. This book will try to answer the question, "How shall I put my pupil in this condition?" The author's advice is, "Don't try to teach a class until they are 'teachable.'"

The teacher must learn the value of bringing herself into the lesson. If she is cross, tired, or her mind filled with thoughts foreign to the lesson, she would better try to leave herself out; if, on the other hand, she is filled with a desire to work for more than money she can fill the position quite acceptably.

Try to make the work simple. Try to make the commands plain. Be sure you are understood by your pupils. These are a few of the very important axioms that should guide you. The young graduate often begins at the wrong end; she has in her mind the latest teaching of her own faculty, she has forgotten the earlier and simpler advice, and so she begins with what she learned last.

The author has used in his teaching a platform; this will form the basis of the chapters that are to follow. A portion of this platform is given below. The discussion of each portion will be found on the pages mentioned.

PLATFORM.

These points will be taken into consideration:

1. Why do we teach? Page 115.

2. What shall we teach?
3. How shall we teach?

Why do we teach gymnastics?

Because the needs of the people demand it.

What are the needs? Page 115.
1. Better health.
2. Greater strength, proportionately distributed.
3. Better physiques.
4. Grace of movement.
5. Self-control and self-reliance.
6. Nerve and brain training.
7. Memory exercises.
8. Mental rest.
9. Recreation.

What shall we teach?
1. Exercises that meet the above requirements.
2. Exercises that promote dexterity and accuracy of motion.
3. Exercises that make the body a better servant of the will.
4. Exercises that induce morality and require obedience.
5. Exercises that demand acute observation.
6. Exercises based upon physiological laws.
7. Exercises founded upon simple principles.
8. Exercises that are safe and progressive.
9. Exercises that are interesting to pupils.
10. Exercises that may be given in the class-room.
11. Exercises that are amenable to the laws of pedagogy.
12. The care of the thorax — "How to breathe." Page 134.
13. What common physical defects are. Page 149.
14. How to overcome these physical defects.
15. How to stand. Page 183.
16. How to walk. Page 153.

INTRODUCTION.

17. How to sit.
18. How to run.
19. How to develop the parts of the body mentioned below.
    (1) Neck. Page 122.
    (2) Shoulders. Page 130.
    (3) Arms, wrists, and hands. Page 124.
    (4) Thorax, and its contents. Page 134.
    (5) Back and spine.
    (6) Waist and abdomen.
    (7) Legs and ankles. Page 123.

Each part will be treated and classified as follows:
1. Definition and divisions.
2. Normal position or condition.
3. Defects.
4. Cause of these defects.
5. Results of these defects.
6. Treatment.
7. Results of treatment on the parts themselves.
8. On circulation, respiration, digestion, and nerves.
9. Secondary effects of treatment.
10. Æsthetic gymnastics.

Exercises are primary or secondary. See page 14.

The motions are slow, medium, or rapid.

Exercises are classified under an alphabet of twenty motions (see page 158):

1. Stepping.
2. Charging.
3. Lunging.
4. Hopping.
5. Reverse charge.
6. Swaying.
7. Swinging.
8. Turning or twisting.
9. Raising and lowering.
10. Bending and straightening.
11. Thrusting.
12. Rolling.
13. Opening and closing.
14. Slapping.
15. Stamping.
16. Circling.
17. Percussing.
18. Shrugging.
19. Placing.
20. Breathing.

So far as practicable the laws of Ling will govern the arrangement of exercises. They are:

1. Introductory, or order movements.
2. Leg   "
3. Head and neck   "
4. Arm   "
5. Balance   "
6. Back or shoulder "
7. Abdominal   "
8. Side waist   "
9. Jumping or running "
10. Slow leg   "
11. Breathing   "

For a description of the day's order see page 57.

The author has requested Jakob Bolin, the instructor in Swedish gymnastics in the Anderson Normal School, in New Haven, and the Chautauqua School of Physical Education, to prepare a chapter on what is known as the Swedish day's order—an excellent arrangement applied to gymnastic movements, and one that is now being generally adopted by the American teachers. There are reasons for placing the movements as they are, and inasmuch as the author wishes to present this matter to the American teachers, he has asked this Swedish authority to write the chapter. The words, therefore, are just as they come from Mr. Bolin's pen.

The Swedish theory is, perhaps, more nearly perfect than that of any other system of gymnastics. The American ideas have been modified and influenced more by the views of the Swedes than by the opinions of any other people. It is not probable that the Swedish system, as it is, will be universally adopted in this country, but there is no question about the influence

INTRODUCTION. 13

that it will have upon our methods. The day's order is used by the author in his teaching at Yale and at Chautauqua. There is some doubt in the minds of those who have tested the subject whether the order of movements will stand close investigation. The author is friendly to the Swedish system, but has made a few experiments upon the position of exercises in the day's order. One of these tests will be given in the chapter devoted to the placing of the jumping exercises, slow leg, and breathing movements. It has been noticed that the various representatives of the Ling system do not agree upon many of the details in their system.

Mr. Henry S. Anderson, instructor of gymnastics at the Yale Gymnasium, has assisted me by acting as a model for the illustrations. Mr. Otto Monahan, the clerk in the Yale Gymnasium, has also assisted me in this way.

TERMS.

THE attention of the teacher will be called at various times to certain names. It is necessary that she should understand the meaning of the phrases to be used. It is the desire of the instructor that one term shall not have a number of different meanings, but shall refer to only one kind of exercise.

Medical Gymnastics. An arrangement of exercises for remedying or curing organic diseases, functional disorders, or any bodily complaint that may be helped by specific, passive, or active means.

Educational Gymnastics. A plan of exercises designed for persons who enjoy moderate health, but whose bodily needs require more general training than that given in the specific work of Medical Gymnastics. School gymnastics are educational.

Free Gymnastics. Exercises that are given without appliances.

Light Gymnastics. Exercises in which light apparatus, such as bells, clubs, wands, etc., are used.

Heavy Gymnastics. Exercises on the bars, bucks, rings, etc.

Military Gymnastics. Are those which more especially refer to marching and tactics.

Æsthetic Gymnastics. Are exercises that pertain to the beautiful. Delsarte work would be of this character. Artistic gymnastics are included under this heading.

Corrective Gymnastics. Are those which are given for curing common physical defects.

Developing Work. That which is given to build up any special part of the body.

Free, Light, Heavy, Corrective, and Developing work are forms of Educational Gymnastics.

Primary Exercises. Are those in which the member of the body directly affected is used.

Secondary Exercises. Are those which bring into action other parts of the body than the one to be especially developed.

A Simple Exercise. Is one calling into action one part of the body.

A Double Exercise. Is one where two parts of the body are used in the same direction.

A Compound Exercise. Is made with one or more members of the body in the same or different directions.

Common Base. Heels touching, toes turned out at an angle of about 60°.

Narrow Base. Heels and toes touching.

Wide Base. Feet separated from four to eighteen inches.

Hips Firm. Hands on the hips.

Neck Firm. Hands touching back of neck.

Letter "y." See page 139.

When the arms are held shoulder high to the side, or out, the palm of the hand may be down, to the front, or up. The term that we use for the first position, viz., Arms out, and palm of the hand down, is, Arms out, *a*. If the palm of the hand is turned to the front, we would say, Arms out, *b*. If the palm is up, the position is described as Arms out, *c*. In the same way we describe the position of the arms when front or up. These terms can also be applied to the exercises taken with the dumb bells.

CHAPTER I.

OPINIONS OF EDUCATORS ON EDUCATION.

THERE is not at the present time any work in the English language chiefly devoted to methods of teaching gymnastics. There are numerous publications on the art or the science of teaching mental branches, but nothing on the subject of bodily training. The teacher is a teacher, whether she molds the body or mind, and it is very necessary that every instructor understand some of the principles of imparting knowledge to others. One who drills a class of children in the Sunday-school should know *how to* teach. The person placed in charge of a large gymnasium must each day instruct pupils and impart knowledge. Of two teachers who have the same amount of material to use, the one who understands the art of teaching will produce the best and quickest results.

For nearly ten years it has been the good fortune of the author to be called upon to teach teachers, both in summer and winter normal classes of gymnastics. These lessons have been given in many parts of the United States and in portions of Canada. During this time there has been ample opportunity to study the methods used by many of the physical directors of both sexes. One would be surprised at the variety of plans or ways adopted by these teachers, a majority of whom are specialists in their work. True, some of them have graduated from teachers' institutes or normal schools devoted to mental training, and are consequently acquainted with the principles of teaching. A few of this number have applied these principles to gymnastics, but the remainder of them seem to think that the elements of pedagogy are applicable only to mental branches. There are too many men and women teaching gymnastics who know nothing of the art or science of teaching; consequently, their efforts are greater than they should be, and the results of their work are not what they would be if better methods were used by them.

At the present time, when the interest in gymnastics is greater than ever before, the market is filled with books on physical education. These works contain many drills and arrangements of exercises which are more or less helpful, but there is no work devoted exclusively to the science or art of applying principles. The object of this manual is to prepare a series of helps for the teacher of physical training—a manual that will be to her what the work on pedagogy is to the teacher of mental branches. The author has made a study of the various works by authorities upon the subject, and has at times quoted freely from these sources. The instructor who reads one good work on pedagogy will find that it contains the gist of many others.

Whether teaching is a science or an art will not be discussed here. It is not of so much importance. There will be given in this work a list of good books, in which the reader can find chapters pertaining to these two questions. That one ought to be a good teacher of gymnastics if she teaches at all is true ; that the opinions, advice, and experience of others should guide her is equally true. A good book may be approved, but if such a work is recommended it too often follows that it is never read. A few opinions of educators have been culled from different sources and are given in this chapter. By this plan the teacher does not feel obliged to purchase new publications, draw them from the city library, or go to any extra trouble to ascertain what others think and say.

A child is taught by one of these three principles: perspective faculty, the expressive faculty, the reflective faculty. Herbert Spencer says: "Educational systems are not made, but grow, and within brief periods growth is insensible." This is truly applicable to the teaching of gymnastics. There has been a steady growth within the last five years, and this growth must continue. Mr. Seldon of St. Louis says: "No matter how limited the strictly scientific domain of education is considered to be, it cannot be denied that there is such a science, and it should be mastered before the practical duties of teaching are assumed." The school-teacher must remember that like begets like, and that as she is, so the school will be. She must be willing to assume the duties and responsibilities of her position. Remember that pupils are at school the first day to study the new teacher, not the lesson. The author remembers the little school in a country town in Illinois, not far from the Mississippi River, where he was first called to teach. The first hour was the most trying one ; he did not know what to do, what to say, or just what the start should be. The result was that the first day's teaching was not satisfactory to the school-directors nor to the teacher, but it seemed to be so to the pupils, because they had a good time. It has been said that husbands who start in their matrimonial career as lieutenants never receive promotion, and that a teacher is rarely promoted in the school in which she has not earned her position at the close of the first day.

This is just as true of teaching gymnastics as it is of teaching the other branches. Professor Bain says: "The teaching method is arrived at in various ways. One principal mode is experience in the work. This is the inductive, or practical course. Another mode is deduction from the laws of the human mind. This is the deductive, or theoretical course. The third and best mode is to combine the two, rectify empirical teaching by principles, and to qualify deductions from principles by practical experience." Mr. J. R. Blackston, one of Her Majesty's inspectors of schools in England, says: "The least gifted may take heart when he bethinks him that success in school management depends mainly on watchful and unremitting attention to little details and grappling with every difficulty as it arises. It is not necessary to decide how much development is possible for the human race in time. The question to be settled is, Can man be raised to a higher plane, physically, intellectually, and morally, and may his upward tendency become stronger and more controlling as he advances?"

The art of school-teaching, or teaching gymnastics, consists in the skilful application of the great body of rules and methods deduced from science, observation, experience, and practice. Dr. Dickinson says: "Successful teaching is the product of knowledge, skill, and experience. The teacher must have a good knowledge of the facts he is to teach, of the sciences which rest upon them, and of the end to be secured by school-work. He must have skill in applying his method, or he will fail to awaken right ideas, or he will do for the pupil what the pupil should do for himself, or he will talk too much, or teach what is not worth knowing. He must have experience, or he will be liable to violate all the principles of good teaching in attempting to apply them." Mill says: "The discipline that does good to the mind is that in which the mind is active and not passive. The secret of developing the faculties is to give them much to do and much inducement to do it." In a conversation with Professor Hughes of Canada, at Chautauqua, during the season of 1892, he said, after watching the classes for an hour: "My criticism of the present method of teaching gymnastics would be that the teacher does too much for the scholars, while the pupils merely imitate or copy." Would not gymnastics produce better results if they were so planned and so taught that the scholar would not only think, but would act, depending upon himself? The Swedes claim that this is one of the strong arguments in favor of their system of physical education. It is not well for the teacher to do too much for the scholar, neither is it wise to always lead or give too many commands. Pupils will soon form the habit of depending entirely upon the leader.

The teacher must be fit for more than the thing she has to do. "If she is not too large for the place, she is too small for it." The teacher should appreciate the value of a general knowledge, and understand that much of her success depends upon the study of the child or of the pupil. Too little attention is paid to this part of the education of the teacher. She seems to fall into a habit, or, as has been said, "to get into a rut." It is hard to change habits that have been formed by years of practice and experience. The one who notices and studies will be better able to instruct children, to deal with them, than one who is satisfied to stand before the class, give a cut-and-dried lesson, and who has not at the end of each day learned or taught something new.

There is no question about the value of methods of teaching in gymnastics. The teacher should begin at the beginning; but the question arises, What is the beginning? In the first place, the teacher should understand why gymnastics are taught.

The reader will notice that most of the advice is given as if to those who are in the habit of teaching children. This is so. The teacher of a child is more apt to be able to instruct adults than the instructor of adults to teach children.

It is an axiom in the art of teaching that it is what the child does for himself and by himself, under wise guidance, that educates him. Tyndall says: "The exercise of the mind, like that of the body, depends for its value upon the spirit in which it is accomplished. The child should be told as little as possible, but induced to discover as much as possible." The unskilled teacher blunders along as if the great educators Mill, Spencer, Froebel, and Pestalozzi had never lived. He recognizes no educational authority but himself. He teaches in the good old way handed down by imitation from the past, and is a law unto himself. Carlyle says: "My teachers were hidebound pedants, without knowledge of man's nature or of boys', or of aught save lexicons." This rule applies forcibly to teachers of gymnastics, to those liable to be placed in the list mentioned by Carlyle.

As is the teacher, so is the school—a maxim that has been often quoted from John Philbrick, the ex-superintendent of the Boston schools. The teacher should avoid recasting everything in the mold of his own ideas. He is in danger of overestimating his powers, because he is seldom questioned in his assertions, the child is not given an opportunity to discuss, arguing does not take place.

Attention is called to some of the main principles of Ratich. With a few modifications they represent the views of that band of educational innovators who came into the field at his time and later. Among them we find Comenius, Locke, Rousseau, Basedow, Pestalozzi, Froebel, and Jacotot. The principles which will be of assistance to the teacher of gymnastics are these:

First. Everything after the order and course of nature, for everything unnatural, violent, and forced is hurtful, both in teaching and learning, and in fact enfeebles nature.

Second. One thing at a time, for nothing hinders the exercise of the understanding more than the attempt to grasp many things at once.

Third. One thing again and again repeated. What is often repeated is clearly and profoundly conceived of by the understanding, for it is incredible what can be accomplished by the frequent repetition of one thing.

Fourth. Everything without coercion, for through coercion and blows children learn to hate study.

Fifth. Nothing is learned by rote, for in learning by rote the attention is fixed on the words and not on the ideas ; but if a thing is thoroughly grasped by the understanding the memory retains it without further trouble.

Sixth. Uniformity of plan in all things, for this is a help to the understanding. There must be plan, method, and system.

Seventh. Everything through experimental analysis, for bare authority is of no value in the absence of cause and reason.

These are some of the principles of Ratich. This representative of the education of the innovators believed that his plans would produce the best results ; he aimed especially at making education a real development and training of the mind, while the development of the bodily powers was also put forward as an important object.

"Froebel is the first teacher to whom it has occurred to convert what is usually considered the waste steam of childish activities and energies into the means of fruitful action ; to utilize what has hitherto been looked upon as unworthy of notice, and, moreover, to accomplish this object, not only without repressing the naturally free spirit of childhood, but by making that free spirit the very instrument of his purpose." "At the same time the bodily powers—hands, feet, muscles, senses—under the influence and impulse of companionship, are more actively exercised, and the health of the constitution thereby promoted, while a larger and better opportunity is supplied for learning the resources of the mother tongue." (That is, when the children are gathered in a kindergarten.) Payne pictures Froebel watching a group of children at play, and reaching this conclusion: "Such, then, appear to be the manifold meanings of the boundless spontaneous activity that I witness. But what name, after all, must I give to the totality of the phenomena exhibited before me? I must call them play. Play, then, is spontaneous activity ending in the satisfaction of the natural desire of the child for pleasure—for happiness. Play is the natural, the appropriate business and occupation of the child left to his own resources. The child that does not play is not a perfect child. He wants something—sense, organ, limb, or generally what we imply by the term health—to make up our ideal of a child. The healthy child plays—plays continually—cannot but play. . . . . I see that these children delight in movement; they are always walking or running, jumping, hopping, tossing their limbs about, and, moreover, they are pleased with rhythmical movement. I can contrive motives and means for the same exercise of the limbs, which shall result in increased physical power, and consequently health—shall train the children to a conscious and measured command of their bodily functions, and at the same time be accompanied by the attraction of rhythmical sound through song or instrument."

A few lines from this famous teacher are quoted not so much for the benefit of the pupil as for that of the teacher herself. Any one giving lessons in physical training will be benefited by carefully considering the advice which may be found in the method of universal instruction. Payne sums up the principles of Jacotot, in part, when he represents him as saying: "I am to be the guide and friend, not the bearer, of my pupil. The journey we are to make together he must make on his own legs, not mine. 'Use legs and have legs,' that is the maxim for our practice; not use mine that he may gain the free use of his own; but so use his own now, that by labor and discipline they may become strong, robust, and well developed, and thus be prepared for the ensuing journey of life. In brief, (1) learn; (2) repeat; (3) reflect; (4) verify. This is the method of Jacotot—of the Universal Instruction."

Writing of Dr. Arnold, of Rugby, Payne says: "The bright example of excellence in the personal character or the work of a successful teacher ought to be, must be, operative on the character and work of every teacher who carefully and admiringly studies it. In the case before us, what ought to have taken place has taken place, for it is beyond a doubt that Arnold's life as an educator has greatly influenced the professional lives of other educators. . . . . How important this is must be acknowledged by the personal experience of every teacher now before me, for it is not merely what we do, but what we by our example cause others to do, that really defines our power. Every one of us is continually, though quite unconsciously, photographing his characteristic features on the minds of those around him, with a force proportioned to the light upon the object and the proper action of the receiving surface."

Speaking of Pestalozzi, Mr. Payne says: "In spite, then, of his patent disqualification in many respects for the task he undertook, in spite of his ignorance of even common subjects—for he spoke, read, wrote, and ciphered badly, and knew next to nothing of classics or science—in spite of his want of worldly wisdom, of any perception and exact knowledge of men and of things, in spite of his being merely an elementary teacher; through the force of his all-conquering love, the nobility of his heart, the resistless energy of his enthusiasm, his firm grasp of a few first principles, his eloquent exposition of them in words, his resolute manifestation of them in deeds, he stands forth among educational reformers as the man whose influence on education is wider, deeper, more penetrating than that of all the rest—the prophet and sovereign of the domain in which he lived and labored."

Pedagogy and Education. "Many writers still confound pedagogy with education. There is more than a shade of difference between these two terms. Pedagogy, so to speak, is the theory of education, and education the practice of pedagogy. Just as one may be a rhetorician without being an orator, so one may be a pedagogue—that is, may have a thorough knowledge of the rules of education—without being an educator—without having practical skill in the training of children."—PAYNE.

Compayre uses the terms pedagogy and pedagogue in

the senses given. A writer who discusses educational questions from the theoretical point of view is a pedagogue, and his treatise is a work on pedagogy ; while a man who directs educational affairs without actually teaching, as a superintendent of public instruction or of schools, is an educator. Education in its theoretical or scientific aspect is pedagogy, while in its practical aspect, or in its art phase, it is educational.

The Relation of Pedagogy to Psychology. As the physician ought to know the organs of the body which he treats, and their functions, the farmer the nature of the soil he cultivates, the sculptor the qualities of the marble he chisels and of the clay which he kneads, so the teacher cannot do without the knowledge of the laws of the mental organization.

" In truth, the rules for teaching are but the laws of psychology applied, transformed into practical maxims, and tested by experience. Psychology is the basis of all the practical sciences which have to do with the moral faculties of man ; but the other sciences which are derived from psychology treat of but certain energies of the human soul—logic of thought, æsthetics, of the sentiment of the beautiful, ethics of the soul. Pedagogy alone embraces all faculties of the soul, and should put under contribution the whole of psychology."—PAYNE.

" The purpose of education is to give to the body and soul all the beauty and all the perfection of which they are capable."—PLATO.

" Education is the development in man of all the perfection which his nature permits."—KANT.

" To educate a child is to put him in a condition to

fulfil as perfectly as possible the purpose of his life."— DE SAUSSURE.

"Education includes whatever we do for ourselves and whatever is done for us by others for the express purpose of bringing us nearer to the perfection of our nature."—MILL.

"Education is preparation for complete living."— HERBERT SPENCER.

"Education is at once the art and the science of guiding the young and of putting them in a condition, by the aid of instruction, through the power of emulation and good example, to obtain the triple good assigned to man by his religious, social, and national destination." —NIEMEYER.

"Education is the harmonious development of the physical, intellectual, and moral faculties."—DENZEL.

"Education is the process by which one mind forms another mind, and one heart another heart."—JULES SIMON.

"Education is the sum of the intentional actions by means of which man attempts to raise his fellows to perfection."—MARION.

"Education is the sum of the efforts whose purpose is to give to man the complete possession and correct use of his different faculties."—JOLY.

"The end of education is to render the individual as much as possible an instrument of happiness to himself, and hence to other beings."—MILL.

"Education is the art of bringing up children and of forming men."—ROUSSEAU.

Chauvet says: "Whoever undertakes the education of another should begin by completing his own."

CHAPTER II.

OPINIONS OF EDUCATORS ON PHYSICAL EDUCATION.

OUR young teachers are frequently called upon to argue in favor of physical training. They are made to feel that their own opinions do not carry enough weight and that the reasoning of modern educators is not sufficiently cogent. A few pages are therefore set aside for the opinions of some of the world's greatest teachers. It is gratifying that these expressions are favorable to rational gymnastics.

The teacher is urged to read Spencer on education; his writings on this and other phases of training are inspiring. The author has looked through the history of education, going as far back as the Greeks, and has selected a few opinions from the representatives of different schools.

Physical Training Among the Greeks. The following passage, which is taken from Xenophon's Memorabilia, quoted by Professor Mahaffy, will give the teacher an idea of the value which was placed upon the care of the body by this wonderful nation. The teacher who is anxious to read the entire quotation, together with others, is referred to the work of Professor Mahaffy. Socrates meets a young man, one of his friends, and seeing that he is in poor bodily condition, reproves him. Among other things, he says: "Moreover, these things [*i. e.*, the care of the body] are not to be neglected in private life because the state does not happen to be engaged publicly in warlike operations. They require, on the other hand, no less attention in times of peace. I would have you know that neither in any other struggle nor in any kind of practical life, will you get on worse because you have brought your body into good condition, for the body is useful in all pursuits which men engage in, in all matters in which the body is useful it is of great importance to have it in the best possible condition. And even in those things in which you may think the body is less useful, namely, in intellectual pursuits, who does not know that, even in these, many men fall into great aberrations through not possessing good bodily health? Nay, weakness of memory, low spirits, ill temper, even insanity, often penetrate the minds of many persons so deeply, through their bad physical condition, as to cast out and dispossess knowledge itself. There is a great security, on the other hand, for those whose bodies are in good condition. They run no risk of suffering any such evils through a low physical condition. Rather it is natural that good bodily health conduces to the very contrary of those evils which arise from bad health. What is there that any reasonable man may not undergo for the sake of securing the opposite of these evils which I have spoken of? It is disgraceful that any one, through want of attention to these matters, should grow old without seeing what sort of a man he can become by making his body as well developed and robust as possible, and this no one can know who does not pay proper attention to these things, for they do not come of their own accord and unsought."

I have quoted at length from the old philosopher, because I wish to speak of the physical condition of the Greeks themselves. One who has made a study of the history of education will be impressed with the fact that the greatest and most successful nations in the world have been those who have regularly cared for the body. Not much is known of the early Chinese, Indian, Egyptian, and Persian education, although we may learn more of the Jewish education by looking into the history of this people. It is not until we pass on to Greek education that we find the most splendid types of high intellectual order that the world has ever produced.

The first duty of the Greek boy was to learn his letters, which was coincident with learning to swim; so that we hear the saying: " 'One who knows neither swimming nor his letters' was the Greek term for an ignoramus." At the age of fourteen the Greek boy would have begun to devote himself to the practice of athletics. The ardor shown in their pursuit by both the Greeks and the Romans is often used as an argument for our devotion to these sports at the present time. There is no doubt that this double attention to the welfare of the body caused the Greeks to become "the most beautiful, as well as the most gifted of mankind."

The Greeks, while they prized athletic distinction, did not hold the professional athlete in high honor. Euripides denounced the race of athletes in strong language. The enthusiasm shown by Homer and Pindar for bodily strength had become weaker in the days of Pericles. Gymnastics and music were closely associated. It has been said that if a Greek youth had by continuous practice become stronger than a bull, more truthful than the godhead, wiser than the most learned Egyptian priest, his fellow-citizens would shrug their shoulders at him in contempt if he did not possess what a series of gymnastics and music alone can give—a sense of gracefulness and proportion. Plato wished that the years from seventeen to twenty could be devoted to athletics as a preparation for the art of war. The first part of the translation quoted above, in which Socrates discusses the subject with his friends, was devoted to the preparation for war, and not for peace.

Aristotle made his order of education, first bodily, second morally, third scientific. He says: "First in education will come gymnastics; but this is intended to make men athletes, not to develop brute force. It is to produce courage, which is a mean between the unbridled wildness of the animal and the sluggishness of the coward. Too much weight must not be given to athletics, lest the child be spoiled; body and mind must not be hard worked at the same time. Gymnastics are only regarded as a preparation for the education of the soul. This is greatly assisted by music." To-day our young men make gymnastic ability the end itself, and not the means.

Roman and Early Christian Education. The Roman education was, in distinction from that of the Athenian, eclectic. This term "eclectic" was used then and is used now, and is an epithet which in itself denotes "chosen from others," and is therefore not original and self derived. "It is the very mark or stamp of a practical mind to gather from every quarter that which will aid its own purposes; therefore, if its own resources are insufficient or unsuitable, to avail itself freely of the resources of others. The Romans have been reproached, and justly, with a want of originality in thinking, but they cannot be reproached with indifference to the originality of others."

A statement has been made by a well-known gymnastic instructor derogatory to the teacher who chooses the best from every system. I must take issue with the one who makes this statement. In the first place, he certainly could not expect us to choose that which was not good in any system. He must know that the American people are independent, original, and ingenious enough to ultimately create a system; that they are somewhat like the Romans, and will borrow from others; that they will never adopt bodily the system of gymnastics recommended by the Germans, Swedes, or the authors of Delsartism; and that they will mold their views and their opinions by the experience, advice, and wisdom of others. Therefore, I say to the young teacher of gymnastics, until this time comes you are to take the best from other systems; certainly not the worst, nor even the parts that are fairly good.

In finishing the chapter devoted to Greek and Roman education, let me quote from Browning, who says, in his educational theories: "The Greek and Roman ideals are the complement of each other. On the one side, man, beautiful, active, clever, receptive, emotional, quick to feel and to show his feeling, to argue, to refine; greedy of the pleasures of the world, if a little neglectful of its duties, fearing restraint as an unjust stinting of the bounty of nature, inquiring into every secret, strongly attached to the things of this life but elevated by an unabated striving after the highest ideal. On the other side, man, practical, energetic, eloquent, tinged but not imbued with philosophy, trained to spare neither himself nor others, reading and thinking only with an apology, ... best engaged in leading armies through unexplored deserts, establishing roads, fortresses, settlements, as the results of conquest, or in ordering and superintending the slow, certain, and utter annihilation of every enemy of Rome. Has the Christian world ever surpassed this type? Can we produce anything by education in modern times, except by combining, blending, and modifying the self-culture of the Greek and the self-sacrifice of the Romans?"

During the age of chivalry, which followed the Roman education, attention was paid to a curriculum of seven sciences. The young squire had his own seven accomplishments to learn, viz. : reading, swimming, shooting with the bow, boxing, hunting, chess-playing, and verse-making. It will be seen from this that attention was paid to outdoor sports, and something to the care of the body.

The Reformers. It will be well to mention one or two of the reformers who paid strict attention to the care of the body and who were at the same time molders of the modern education. Luther would have things, as well as words, taught in the school—mathematics, history, logic, gymnastics, and music. "Music," he says, "is the best of all the arts. It dispels the sorrow of the breast. If a schoolmaster does not know music I have nothing to say to him. Music is a beautiful, divine gift of God, and next to theology." Luther, in his own teaching, closely associates music with gymnastics.

Another of the great reformers was Trotzendorf, rector of the school at Goldberg. In his teaching he was careful to promote the physical education by gymnastic exercises. He allowed his boys to run and wrestle in the playground, praised the successful, blamed the bunglers, and yet made a special law forbidding them to bathe in the summer or go upon the ice in the winter and to divert themselves with snowballing. This seems inconsistent, and indicated the prevailing defective views at that time upon the subject of physical training. Melancthon says that Trotzendorf was as much born to drill a school as Scipio Africanus to drill an army. If, in the opinion of such a man as Melancthon, he was competent, we may connect the care of the body with the success that his scholars attained.

Montaigne says: "I would have the youth's outward behavior and mien and the disposition of his limbs formed at the same time with his mind. It is not a soul, it is not a body, that we are training up, but a man, and we ought not to divide him."

The views of Locke on physical education will be interesting because, with few exceptions, they are in accord with the rules for athletic training at the present day. He was a partisan of what was then called, and is now frequently termed, the "hardening system"; but, as another author has tersely put it, some of his plans would very soon harden many out of the world. His precepts for physical training do not seriously conflict with the modern practice of hygiene, except in one or two matters about which he had peculiar notions or, as the modern phrase is, fads. His views may be summed up in this paragraph, taken from Mr. Quick:

"And thus I have done with what concerns the body and life, which reduces itself to these few and easily observed rules: plenty of open air, exercise, and sleep, plain diet, no wine or strong drink, and very little or no physic, not too warm or strait clothing, especially the head and feet kept cool, and the feet often used to cold water and exposed to wet." Here the only point open to criticism is the strange notion of keeping the children's feet cold and wet, which would now be considered a dangerous blunder.

Rousseau says that there are two important points to be kept in mind; the first, that to teach children wisely and efficiently we must know child nature; the second, that without such knowledge we cannot really sympathize with that nature. He says: "Exercise, therefore, not only the physical strength but also the senses that direct it, make the best possible use of each, and verify the impressions of one by those of another. To learn to think, therefore, we should learn to exercise our limbs, senses, organs, since these are the instruments of our intelligence, and in order to make the best use of these instruments it is necessary that the body which produced them should be robust and healthy. Thus, so far is a sound instinct from being independent of the body that it is owing to a good constitution that the operations of the mind are effected with ease and certainty."

The naturalist Rabelais lays great stress upon physical

exercise. The list of physical exercises which Gargantua was called upon to perform is given with the usual enthusiasm of this author. Of the chief points upon which Rabelais insists, viz., the teaching through the senses, independence of thought, training for practical life, equal development of mind and body, general treatment, and improved methods, the last three are in close touch with physical or bodily training.

According to Milton, the first step in the education of pupils is to make them "despise and scorn all their childish and ill-taught qualities, to delight in manly and liberal exercises, to infuse into their young hearts such ingenious and noble ardor as will not fail to make many of them renowned and matchless men." It will be noticed also that with Milton, amusement, emulation, bodily skill, cheerfulness of bright companionship, are all associated with physical training. He recommended "the art of the sword, to guard, to strike safely with edge or point, to practice in all the locks and grips of wrestling, which exercises will keep pupils healthy, strong, and well in breath. It is also the likeliest means to make them grow large, tall, and to inspire them with a gallant and fearless courage."

"Physical training and drill should be a part of the regular business of school. There is no real difficulty about teaching the drill and the simpler kinds of gymnastics. If something of the kind is not done, the physique which has been and still is, on the whole, a grand one, will become in the great towns as extinct as a dodo."—HUXLEY.

"Play is the development of the human mind in its

first effort to make acquaintance with the outward world."—FROEBEL.

"No perfect brain ever crowns an imperfectly developed body."—CLARK.

Let the teacher of gymnastics take a lesson from the few words of this great teacher of children, the champion of the kindergarten. If Froebel's success was due to his knowledge of the human nature of the child and the turning of his work into play, the teacher of gymnastics should make use of this principle.

"Health is wealth."—EMERSON.

"Gymnastic exercises give grace and beauty to the body, and good training to the mind."—DICKINSON.

"The cold, formal, precise, unsympathetic teacher should never set foot on the playground. An owl frightens singing birds. The only teachers who succeed well in drilling children in calisthenics, gymnastics, or games, are those who can enter into the spirit of girlhood or boyhood."—SWETT.

A Quotation from a Program of French Instruction. "The purpose of physical education is not merely to furnish the body and strengthen the constitution of the child, by placing him in the most favorable hygienic conditions, but it should also give him, at an early age, qualities of deftness and agility with manual dexterity, and with promptness and certainty of mind; which, valuable for every one, are more particularly necessary for pupils in the common schools, the most of whom are destined for manual occupations."

"Gymnastics do not labor merely for the future, by enlarging and strengthening the chest, by giving suppleness to the limbs, and by contributing to the health of the child. Exercise acts immediately upon the state of the body, whose forces it renews, and upon the nervous system, which it tempers. It has a happy effect upon studies, because it reëstablishes the equilibrium in the organism, and at the same time gives the mind more vigor and elasticity. Gymnastics, like play, take the child wearied, enfeebled by study and cerebral effort, and restore him to intellectual labor refreshed and active; but it will do this on one condition—that we can never pass the limit beyond which fatigue has begun. An excessive exercise of the body makes the mind inert, while moderate exercise reanimates and refreshes."—*Payne.*

Play. Herbert Spencer says: "Happiness is the most powerful of tonics. By accelerating the circulation of the blood, it facilitates the performance of every function, and so tends alike to increase health when it exists, and to restore it when it is lost. Hence the essential superiority of play in gymnastics.

"Play in the open air, which invites to jump, to run without interruption, to shout at the top of the voice; which causes the blood to circulate vigorously and to give color to the cheeks—this is the agent, of all others, for physical development. The English and the Americans well know this, and we have play as a national institution."

Froebel says: "We should not consider play as a frivolous thing. On the contrary, it is a thing of profound signification. By means of play the child expands in joy as the flower expands when it proceeds from the bud, for joy is the soul of all the actions of that age."

CHAPTER III.

THE ETHICAL ELEMENT IN PHYSICAL TRAINING.

TEACHERS of gymnastics, or "physical educators," as they are sometimes called, do not hold the same opinions regarding the results of their training, the systems they should use, or the methods they should adopt. There are in their profession several "schools," each of which has among its adherents many who are so prejudiced in favor of their own faction that they do not carefully investigate the principles underlying the other schools, or make an honest effort to be fair and just in expressing their opinions.

There is jealousy among the representatives of the various gymnastic systems in America, but it can be said that this feeling exists in all professions and schools. It therefore does not follow that, because we are gymnasts, we need the great ethical element of charity more than others, or that physical education fails to create a feeling of brotherly love. Because of the different opinions expressed by the members of our profession we are, obviously, not unanimous in our views, and as we do not yet agree upon the same results accruing from each system, it may be well to present the objects or aims of the Swedish, German, Delsarte, and "so-called" American systems of physical training. By doing this the ethical element in physical training can be determined as well by the authorities on moral philosophy as by the physical educators. Rational physical training is yet new in the United States, and we are not sure that the results of which we speak will follow. The ethical element has been discussed but little in our schools. In short, ethics is not, though it should be, taught, in our normal training schools of gymnastics.

The general plan of this chapter is this:

1. Ascertain what is meant by the terms physical training; physical education; gymnastics; athletics, etc.; also the objects and aims of the several systems of gymnastics.

2. To find, if possible, what is meant by ethics, and so trace the relationship between the two subjects.

Authorities on the Swedish, German, Delsarte, and American methods have been consulted, so that, in speaking of the aims of these institutions, the author's statements are based upon their expressed opinions.

DEFINITION.—Dr. E. M. Hartwell, the American authority on physical education, in his "Provisional Schematic Study of Leading Topics," says:

" Physical Education as an Expression.

" A. The term is used in :

"(1) *A vaguely general, uncritical, and popular sense*, when it means too much, being made to include matters that belong to personal and school hygiene; *e. g.*: bathing, diet, dress, seating of pupils, ventilation.

"(2) *A semi-general sense*, signifying exercise for the sake of health or recreation or the prevention of mischief, when it means too little, though it is generally so used by school boards and educators.

"(3) *A strictly scientific sense*, based on a critical consideration of demonstrable physiological and psychological effects and relations. Its general and special scientific significations should be distinguished and determined.

"B. *Synonymous terms*, e. g.: physical training; bodily exercise.

"C. *Non-synonymous terms*, e. g.: physical culture; movement cure; society gymnastics; Delsarte exercises.

"Physical Education as a Department of Science.

"A. The essential, universal, necessary factor in all forms of physical training is *neuro-muscular exercise*. It should be critically considered in respect to:

"(a) *Its nature and effects:* (1) Bodily; (2) Mental.

"(b) *Its aims*, which may be: (1) Recreative; (2) Hygienic; (3) Educative; (4) Remedial.

"(c) *Its results*, which are: (1) Anatomical; (2) Physiological; (3) Mental; (4) Moral.

"B. *As a branch of hygeine. Physical training* serves to promote the normal growth and development of:

"(1) *The master tissues and organs;* i. e., muscles, nerves, and brain.

"(2) *The purveyor tissues and organs.*

"(3) *The scavenger tissues and organs.*

"C. *As a pedagogic discipline. Physical training* helps to develop will and intelligence, *i. e.*, the power to know, do, endure, and forbear.

"It lies at the basis of mental and moral training; hence its place should be defined and its value determined in relation to the ends and needs of:

"(1) *Somatic or general bodily training;* e. g.: in the matter of carriage, walking, running, dancing.

ETHICAL ELEMENT IN PHYSICAL TRAINING. 43

"(2) *Language training;* *e. g.:* singing, gesture, speaking, for general and special ends.

"(3) *Manual training;* *e. g.:* writing, drawing, and the use of tools for educational purposes.

"(4) *Industrial training;* for the professional training of skilled workmen.

"(5) *Military training;* *e. g.:* of boys playing at soldiers, of militia, soldiers, and sailors.

"(6) *Normal training;* general and special, in each of the chief departments of education, viz. : in elementary, secondary, superior, and technical education."

Thus, according to so eminent an authority, physical education as a department of science should be critically considered in respect to its results, which are physical, mental, and moral, while as pedagogic discipline it helps to promote will and intelligence.

The objects of the Swedish system, as given by Mr. Skarstrom of the Chautauqua School of Physical Education, are as follows :

"The aim of Swedish gymnastics is to harmoniously train and develop all parts of the body, so as to make it an efficient and obedient servant or tool of the *will*, and to put it in a condition most favorable for the duties and activities of life. In other words, the aim is to improve the condition of the individual in a physical, mental, and moral sense."

1. In pedagogical gymnastics, the training and strengthening of the respiratory and circulatory functions is the first consideration, for those are the fundamental functions of the body, and on them depend the welfare and efficiency of all other functions. The ex-

ercises used are such as will train the strength and efficiency of the heart and lungs and assist their action, and all exercises are excluded that are in any way detrimental to those organs, or that would tend to permanently impede their activity. This we might call the general hygienic object of pedagogical gymnastics—improved nutrition.

2. The exercises in Swedish pedagogical gymnastics tend to correct all faulty and incorrect positions and carriage of the body, the results of bad habits of sitting, standing, or walking, so common especially during the growing age and in school-desk life, and to encourage a correct and healthy growth of the spine and thorax, and a good position and carriage of the shoulders and head.

3. Besides these elements, there also comes in a purely educational feature, a training of the nervous system; for the exercises used are such as to demand exactness of muscular coördination, each movement and position being defined in every detail; the aim being to so train the body that certain groups of muscles, in response to the command of the will, shall by their contraction produce a certain movement and nothing else.

"If to this we add that most of the movements and positions are taken in response to a command requiring an instantaneous execution on a given signal, and when the exercises are serial the rhythm is kept up by the individual's own sense of rhythm, it must follow that alertness of perception, quickness of action, a keen posture sense, a high degree of coördination and power of inhibition—in a word, a greater volitional control and a feeling of being master of one's self, will be the result of the training. In how far this will affect the higher mental qualities, the moral strength, and the general character of the individual has not been ascertained."

Again, the Swedish system works for purity of movement, also for exactness of coördination, which term they sometimes call *grace*. The æsthetic element in the Swedish system has not been fully developed. The teachers try to arouse interest in the work, to create pleasure, and to exert a cheering influence. They claim that the work can be so given that joy and exhilaration will result. These same effects are secured partly in the German and American schools through the aid of music. The Swedish school does not believe in this latter plan.

What are the aims of the German system of gymnastics? This question is well answered by Guts Muth in his "Gymnastics for the Youth of the Fatherland," when he says: "Gymnastics are work in the garb of play. Their aim is to maintain the equilibrium between body and mind." The following are the aims, in detail, as given by the same author:

(*a*) A healthy body, lively and energetic.

(*b*) Manly ruggedness, gained by contact with and exposure to the inclemencies of the outer world, and reasonable and rational training.

(*c*) Uniform and symmetrical development of all the parts.

(*d*) Subtlety and elasticity of body and limbs, in order to cope with difficulties and dangers.

(*e*) Alertness of all the senses.

(*f*) Development and maintenance of a manly courage.

Thus, German gymnastics aim to educate the muscular and nervous systems, the mental faculties, the different senses, so far as possible, bringing the different parts of the body as much as possible under the influence of the *will*.

As for the ends and aims sought, they may be divided into two classes: the physical, and the mental, psychological, and ethical. The physical aims may be briefly summed up as follows: health, strength of body and limb, uniform and symmetrical build, erectness of body and ease of movement, quickness and speed of action, exactness and precision, power of endurance, and graceful and easy carriage. The mental, psychological, and ethical aims are: discipline, will power, manliness, courage, self-reliance, respect for self and others, presence of mind, sense of beauty in form and action, quickness of thought and perception, and last, but not least, love of country—patriotism.*

The following extract gives some of the principles which underlie the ideas of the Delsarte school: "Integrity of mental action and integrity of moral purpose certainly in a degree depend upon integrity of muscle. This is shown by the muscles of those who may be called mentally and morally irresponsible. The muscles of idiots are flaccid, and Charles Dudley Warner tells us how an habitual lack of moral integrity is registered in the weakened tissues of the body, producing what is known as 'criminal muscle.' Gymnastics which promote health of body and muscular development are, it is

---
* Dr. Schmidt.

ETHICAL ELEMENT IN PHYSICAL TRAINING. 47

believed, indirect agencies toward higher ethical conditions; while gymnastics psychologically taught, as in 'Americanized Delsarte Culture,' are direct agencies toward the development of will, judgment, and character. In these psychological gymnastics the correspondence between the inner states—mental and moral—and the outer physical manifestations, is made the basis of the training." *

To summarize, we find that the objects of the different systems of physical training are: better health, better physique, grace, self-control, self-reliance, fortitude, courage, power of endurance, alertness of perception, quickness of action, higher degree of coördination, muscular development, will power, morals. While each school does not describe its objects in the same words, it is plain that most of the results are common to each, in theory if not in practice. There is no American system of physical education, but if one is ever made it will be built upon sound principles, and its growth will be influenced by the experience of the other schools.

We are not now ready to say that physical training will do all that is claimed for it, nor are any of the present systems of gymnastics perfect enough to produce all of the results mentioned. Visitors at the meetings of the American Association for the Advancement of Physical Education comment freely on the fact that among those present, who represent gymnasia in all parts of the country, there are comparatively few well-built men and women, while the appearance of health is not so noticeable as to call attention to any great difference between

---
* Mrs. Emily M. Bishop.

this gathering of the disciples of health and that of the representatives of any other profession. The voices of many of those who read papers or spoke, especially of the women, are noticeably weak ; while pale, thin faces, poor chests, and unevenly developed bodies are not uncommon. These meetings are, however, gatherings of hard-working, hard-thinking, enthusiastic, earnest men and women, who come together to learn how to better care for the bodies of their pupils. It would be a difficult matter to say to which school this or that person belongs, and yet each system is represented by delegates claiming superior advantages for its methods, but not in their own cases showing these advantages. It cannot be denied, however, that the delegates showed intelligence, kindness, self-control, self-reliance ; that they were quick and accurate in their movements, and seemed possessed of more than ordinary will power. The ethical part of their training, or the moral results, were more evident than the purely physical.

It is not always necessary that our men and women have typical physiques to possess the desired ethical elements. The question for discussion is not, "Does physical training produce better physiques, greater strength, and a healthier appearance?" but, "Does it educate those qualities which are allied to, or are a part of, moral philosophy?" Physical training does not do for those who are in constant practice all that we claim for it, but it does not consequently follow that there may not be some day a system that will. The ethical element plays a far more important part in our present schools of gymnastics than is credited to it or recognized by gymnastic teachers. We are apt to admit and pass over too quickly the moral side of physical training, and give our attention to other and more attractive phases—one of which may be the exercises themselves, which are too often considered the end, instead of the means. We value physical education, or, for that matter, any form of education, for what it does; not for what is said of it.

In what way does physical education help the morals? In which of the two, gymnastics or athletics, do we find the ethical element to a greater degree, and what are our reasons for our decisions? If the physical educators are not sure of the results of their efforts, are the moral philosophers sufficiently agreed upon the subject of ethics to decide the question for us if we present our side to the best of our ability?

The object of life is the complete development of all the moral possibilities of man. These possibilities are seven-fold. Man is capable of development physically, æsthetically, intellectually, socially, politically, religiously, and morally. A man who neglects one or more of these natures is one-sided, and the man who develops each one of these natures nearest to its utmost possibility of development comes closer to attaining the object of life.

We know that physical training develops the physical possibility in man. Then, if we accept Prof. B. P. Bowne's views, the first link between ethics and physical training is established. In every system of physical training we find æsthetic gymnastics. We may infer, then, that the second link exists. All gymnastic schools admit that the moral training is helped by the physical. If this is true we may look for still another connection, so that there remains the social, political, religious, and intellectual, although it is claimed that the intellect is developed through physical training. Gymnastics—by this term is meant the work in light and free gymnastics and on apparatus like bars, ropes, etc.—develops courage, prompt decision, self-control, judgment, self-reliance, and fortitude. The dangerous part of gymnastic work could not be done without these virtues, while the falls, slips, and slight accidents teach fortitude.

Football cannot be played by cowards. The rough usage that a young man receives on the field would soon cause him to withdraw if he lacks, what is very essential in this popular game, "sand," which is another name for "will." It is only necessary to examine the scarred bodies of our football players to know that they must bear pain like stoics. The game develops fortitude and courage, great self-control, quick judgment, prompt action, and endurance. In athletics we find the need of endurance, good judgment, and prompt action.

In all gymnastics and athletics, if we want the best results we must obey a cardinal rule, which is, "Be good." The strict laws of training in athletics and gymnastics forbid every kind of vice. They demand the very best care of the body, which is looked upon as a clean, well-tempered instrument governed by a strong will. No form of immorality will be tolerated, while smoking, or even carrying a pipe in the mouth, is forbidden. At the training table the choicest and most strengthening food is served. The conversation is of a healthful kind. Profanity is not allowed.

The athletes avoid company that will tempt them to violate these moral laws. They eat, sleep, and live by themselves. They admit by word and deed that their success depends upon their moral habits as much as upon the regular physical training. It is true that for some of the representatives of the crews, teams, and nines training is a necessary evil, and in their cases there is often a relapse after the season is over, but this does not detract from the weight of the argument that to succeed in athletics one must lead a strictly moral life.

The *morale* of a team depends, to a great extent, upon the captain, but he is generally careful about the example he sets. One outside of college and preparatory school life knows little of the influence which the captain exerts over most undergraduates. They seek his society and while with him obey the unwritten laws. Many of the associates of athletes copy their ways of living; their habits and customs are discussed and imitated by boys in preparatory and secondary schools. It is true that the betting habit is an evil, but this is practiced mostly by those not connected with athletics and gymnastics.

The consensus of opinion is that the moral tone of the athletes is above that of other undergraduates. A Yale man remarks that the habit of training required on the baseball field clung to him after leaving college, so that he was able to discontinue smoking by its aid. An Amherst man states that of the fourteen men on his victorious football team of 1892, eight were of exceptionally high moral character. In the 1891 team the moral tone was even higher. He also insists that the average moral character of Amherst athletes is above that of the undergraduates of the same college. A Williams athlete makes a similar statement. Cowan, the famous Princeton football player, has made the statement that the backbone of their team was made up of moral men, while the reputation of Stagg, Williams, Heffelfinger, and others bears testimony to these statements. This is evidence from athletes themselves.

Our best amateur and professional gymnasts bear witness also to the truth of these statements. The professional gymnast is moral in many cases because it is a means to an end, and that end is—cash. He has never heard of the utilitarian or intuitional schools of ethics. He does right because it brings him the greatest happiness, namely, a big salary. Consequently his living is right because it brings him happiness, according to the "goods ethics." On the other hand, to do right because it is right is nothing to him, so that duty ethics would play no part in his life. We have found that the young man who has trained his body either by athletics or gymnastics has a far greater control over himself and is less liable to commit immoral acts than the one who has not.

This is true, also, with schoolboys. The one who is trained in a gymnasium has greater strength of will to overcome evil habits than the one who has not been so trained. We therefore try to teach small boys not only to care for their bodies, but to associate with health and strength moral ideas. The immoral small boy is often such an expert prevaricator that he can deceive the "very elect." He will listen to advice, but the notes of warning fall on dull ears. This child can be helped in the gymnasium or on the field quicker and better than in any other way. Bodily action is desirable in his case. Without a full, strong, natural action of the bodily functions, which is good for him morally and intellectually, both the moral nature and the mind are clogged. We cannot coerce a boy into being good, but we can surround him with moral influences. Physical training does this. Health of body must tend to promote a healthful mind and heart.

"The character of a man is determined by his supreme choice." He has a strong physical character when he possesses great bodily strength, a strong moral character when he has the power of doing moral acts. What constitutes moral character? There are two elements: first, a strong will, or the power of decision; second, a man must desire and choose the good in preference to evil. Can we show that physical training develops the will, or that the choice of good is influenced by gymnastics and athletics? Professor James of Harvard says: "The will is the power which holds the idea prominently before the mind until it results in action," or, more simply stated, it is the power which commands action. This is shown in every feat of strength and skill in gymnastics, and there is little doubt in my mind but that the will is strengthened and developed by physical training. Regarding the direction in which this force is exerted, it is known that the force may be exerted either in a moral or an immoral direction, and, although a man may be free to choose between good and evil, there are influences that have the power of determining his course of action. These influences are his own physical condition and his environment. A sound body tends to make a man good natured and philanthropic, while De Quincey's opium habit is a classical example of the desperate resorts to which dyspepsia can drive its victims.

Rev. Dr. Munger of Yale College makes this statement:
"When we think, it is not alone the mind that thinks, it is the whole man, and the process begins with the body. The bodily fiber or quality reaches to the thought. You will never get fine thought out of a coarse body. Nor less will you get sound thought out of an unsound body. The bodily condition strikes through and shows itself in the quality of the thought. A vast amount of the poor, illogical, insipid, morbid, extravagant, pessimistic thought that finds its way into books and sermons and conversation has its origin in poor bodies and bad health. The body lies at the basis of success in all respects. A poor body means a poor life all the way up, even to the highest stages of spiritual life. Any religious experience that is connected with a weak or diseased body is to be regarded with suspicion. There can be no healthy thought, no normal feeling, no sound judgment, no vigorous action, except in connection with a sound body. Great minds are often shut up in poor bodies—as Pascal and Cowper, and Carlyle and Amiel— but in each case we make allowance for what is called the personal equation; their opinions are examined in the light of their physical weakness or disease before they are trusted."

The testimony of G. Stanley Hall also is valuable. He says:

"I plead strongly for physical education on the grounds of good morals. I believe that the temptations that assail young people nowadays are to quite an extent those that would not overcome them if their muscles were strong. They are of that insidious, corroding, undermining kind that are somehow or other so prone to creep in as the contractile tissues become relaxed and habitually flabby."

Finally, then, physical education develops moral character, first, by lending its strength to the will; secondly, by directing this strength to moral channels through the influence of a man's own physical nature, through his associates and the purity of the scenes of his work. The minister of the gospel should know more of physical training when teaching ethics; the public school-teacher should know more of both physical training and ethics; while the teacher of gymnastics should know more of ethics.

"The laws of health are the laws of God, and are as binding as the Decalogue."—PARKER.

"The physiology is educating men for manhood and women for womanhood, both for humanity. In this lies the hope of the race."—DR. CLARK.

"Get health, for sickness is a cannibal which eats up all the life and youth it can lay hold of, and so absorbs its own sons and daughters."—EMERSON.

"At college I was taught the motions of the heavenly bodies, as if their keeping in their orbits depended upon my knowing them, while I was in profound ignorance of the laws of health of my own body. The rest of my life was, in consequence, one long battle with exhausted energies."—HORACE MANN.

F. Marion, in speaking on physical education, says: "Physical perfection serves to assure moral perfection. There is nothing more tyrannical than enfeebled organism. Nothing sooner paralyzes the free activity of the reason, the flight of the imagination, and the exercise of reflection, nothing sooner dries up all the sources of thought, than a sickly body, whose functions languish, and for which every effort is a cause of suffering. Then have no scruples, and if you would form a soul which is to have ample development, a man of generous and intrepid will, a workman capable of great undertakings and arduous labors, first, and above all, secure a vigorous organism, of powerful resistance, and muscles of steel."

"Aristotle thought that the highest object of man is the attainment of happiness, and the highest happiness of man is to be reached by perfect virtue. Neither perfect happiness nor perfect virtue can be had without perfect health. The end of life, and therefore of education, is the attainment at once of intellectual, moral, and physical virtue. Boys know well that games conduce, not merely to the physical but to moral health—that in the ball-field boys acquire virtues that no books can give them, such as control of temper, self-restraint, fairness, honor, unenvious approbation of another's success, and all that give and take life which stands a man in such good stead when he goes forth into the world and without which, indeed, success is always maimed and partial."—CHARLES KINGSLEY.

CHAPTER IV.

THE GYMNASTIC DAY'S ORDER.

The object of gymnastics in our schools is primarily a hygienic one: it is an effort to maintain the health of the pupils at the highest possible level, in spite of the evil influences of a too one-sided mental training coupled with the sedentary habits which usually accompany a studious life.

If we exclude from the gymnastic exercises not only those forbidden by the anatomico-mechanical structure of the normal body, but also such as have a tendency to induce injurious positions and make them permanent, we may ascribe a certain hygienic value to every other kind of muscular activity within physiological limits, on account of its stimulating effect on the general nutrition. But the different forms of bodily movements, of course, do not react upon the body in the same manner; some have a decidedly local effect, promoting nutrition in the special parts directly affected by them, while the local result of some other forms is insignificant when compared to the general improvement of the whole system, which accrues from them; and among these latter some act principally through increased general circulation, some principally by improving the respiration, some principally by regulating the nutrition, and so on.

Hence, the gymnastic movements may, according to

their physiological effect, be classified into groups or natural families, into each of which are brought together those movements which in all main features resemble each other, but vary in minor details. When certain effects of gymnastics are found desirable, it is then evident that not all possible movements are to be recommended, nor an indiscriminate, haphazard choice among them; but only such, the effects of which are known to tend strongly in the desired direction. This self-evident truth, which must be one of the cornerstones of all gymnastic work, may be called the *principle of gymnastic selection*.

On the other hand, even if one organ or part of the body, or a few organs or parts of the body, be more in need of the health and strength-giving, or the corrective influence of muscular work, the body as a whole always suffers, to a greater or less extent, by infirmity or deterioration in any particular part, and as a consequence no important family of movements can be altogether overlooked, when we make up a schedule of the gymnastics for a certain individual or a certain class of individuals, even if movements for specific purposes in certain cases must have a prominent place. The whole body, the whole man, must have proper attention. The human being is not a machine which will be kept in the best running condition by the occasional repair of certain independent parts, which together constitute the whole, and of which some may be in need of special attention; but the work must be so arranged that the whole is not forgotten for the sake of its parts. This is the *principle of gymnastic totality*.

THE GYMNASTIC DAY'S ORDER

Closely connected with this is the third principle underlying rational gymnastics, *that of gymnastic unity*, which means that the effects of the different movements used must be considered not only with regard to themselves, but also with regard to all the other movements employed, in such a manner that the effect of the one does not nullify or unduly multiply that of any other. Only by such selection and arrangement may we hope to gain the most favorable results from our work within the shortest possible time.

A list of movements, selected and arranged on these principles, and intended to constitute the gymnastic work during each day of a shorter or longer period of time, until the conditions of the pupils so change with regard to health, strength, control of the body, etc., as to warrant a corresponding change in the movements used, has been called a *gymnastic day's order*.

From what has already been said, it is apparent that the day's order is very variable, according to the desired results and the conditions under which the work is to be given. Its character depends on the most varied circumstances; it is influenced by the general health, age, sex, strength, and other qualities of the pupils, by the time allotted to the work, by the nature of the place where the exercises are given, whether in the schoolroom, in a regularly appointed gymnasium, on a suitable ground in the open air. The instructor must, in order to be successful and to do justice to his pupils, so vary his schedules as to bring them in accord with these and other conditions. There are consequently no fixed and ironclad rules with regard to the composition of the day's order.

But experience shows that in all such institutions where it is especially desirable to benefit from gymnastics, the conditions present important similarities, which make it possible to recommend a certain type of day's order, which can and ought to be more or less strictly adhered to, but which need not, and must not, be slavishly followed. The indications in the different cases decide the necessary deviations from it.

Thus, every day's order is properly prefaced by such preparations as will tend to bring order out of chaos, to put the class under the control of the instructor and enable him without loss of time, rapidly, and with ease to move the whole class or its component parts, divisions, or individuals, to different places, or into different positions, in them or from them to execute the necessary movements. These movements, which are not gymnastic in the same hygienic sense as those which follow, all of which have a definite hygienic purpose, have received the common name, *order movements*, and consist mainly of taking the fundamental positions, alignments, spreading and bringing the class together into different formations, and similar evolutions, often borrowed from military tactics. Besides the object just mentioned, they are also intended to attract the attention of the pupils from the usual mental work to work of a totally different nature, to awake them and put physical life into them. They are, therefore, quick and sharp, requiring a minimum of muscular strength.

When their object is gained, the work is introduced by mild movements to increase the arterial afflux to the muscles, thus relieving the cerebro-spinal system from the congestive tendency created by mental work assisted by more or less cramped postures. If the allotted time permits it, these *introductory movements* consist of a series of free standing movements, embracing simple forms from several of the natural families—head, arm, trunk, and leg movements—among which the *leg movements* are predominant, and are used alone, if the time be short. This predominance of the leg movements is based upon the fact that they bring greater masses of muscles into play than any other form of mild movements, and as a result their "derivative" influence is very marked. They are also used frequently in our daily life, or closely related to forms which are, and the necessary amount of cerebration is therefore comparatively small; which means, with regard to their regulative influence upon the circulation, that no great counteracting power is brought to bear against their derivative effect.

Next follow *tense-bendings*, the type of which is recognized by an evenly distributed, gentle backward curve of the whole body from the feet to the hands, which are extended above the head grasping a firm support behind, upon which, by the full extension of the arms, they execute a push which brings a tension upon the whole front aspect of the body. The effect of this group is far-reaching: the antero-posterior curve in the upper part of the vertebral column, generally exaggerated into deformity by the usual sitting posture, is flattened, which causes the ribs to be spread out in front in a fan shape—an effect which is to some extent increased by the traction exerted upon the sternum and the ribs by the arms through the pectorals; the intervertebral disks, upon the front part of which the usual posture brings a strong pressure supplemented by long-sustained traction on the posterior ligaments, are relieved from this pressure, and in its place a corresponding compression of their hindmost parts and an extension of the anterior ligaments take place. This passive extension concerns, however, not only the anterior vertebral ligaments proper, but reaches also other ligaments and muscles, which in a contracted state serve as ligaments; again, the extension of these muscles, for instance, the intercostal and abdominal ones, which in itself is a means to increase their extensibility, and thus their proper functional ability, causes also an equalization of the circulation by assisting the venous reflux from them; this effect is still more emphasized both by the thoracic aspiration which results from the position, and by the mechanical raising of the diaphragm and abdominal viscera, which are so often congested or suffer from sluggish circulation on account of being pressed down into or toward the pelvis. These are only a few points. It would take a great deal too much space to enumerate all the modes in which the tense-bendings act beneficially.

We now bring in one or more *heave-movements, i. e.*, such in which the body is wholly or partly suspended by means of the hands. If the tense-bendings are looked upon as corrective exercises for the thorax *par excellence*, the heave-movements may be spoken of as educative. The passive expansion which the former cause we find also in this group, though in a far milder degree; but to this is added an active element by which the thoracic cage is lifted by the action of its own muscles, which thereby are to be educated to maintain the correct posture. The pectorals, for instance, contract powerfully toward their humeral attachments, which are made fixed by the posture, and actively lift the sternum and ribs. The increased strength in these muscles, which results from a judiciously progressive use of this class of movements, is of course explained by the increased arterial afflux, while the sedative influence of the movements, which is frequently noticed, probably is due to the increased venous reflux from the head on account of the thoracic aspiration, and from the spine because of its passive extension.

The heave-movements require quite a good deal of muscular strength, whether in their purest form, such as heaving and sinking of the body by means of the arms, or in more mixed types, such as climbing. Some muscular fatigue will therefore result, and we find a necessity to introduce after them such movements as require comparatively little strength. Now our pupils usually have a poor general carriage of their bodies. No movements are better apt to improve them in this respect than the so-called *balancing movements*, which train the powers to maintain the equilibrium in more or less difficult postures, generally upon a small base of support. But these are also movements which require only little muscular strength, and they are therefore introduced here as a relief from the previous groups. While executing these movements, the pupils may rest. Besides, they have a tendency to moderate the accelerated heart action. Their principal effect is the education of the power of coördination, teaching the pupils to send stimuli of correct strength to the correct muscles. The longitudinal muscles running from vertebra to vertebra and principally concerned in keeping this movable pillar of segments in the correct position to maintain its equilibrium, must be properly coördinated to fill their office, for which a well-adjusted cerebration is necessary. And not only they, but the other muscles of the trunk and those of the legs also are implicated in the movements, and their contractions must be finely adjusted. It is just at this place in the day's order that such a work may be best undertaken, because the previous exercises have, as has already been stated, relieved the brain of the impure blood which has collected there during the previous mental work, while the muscular work has not been of such intensity as to cause fatigue of the motor cells or to saturate the general circulation with fatigue stuffs.

Now commences a part which is intended mainly to make permanent the undoing of the evils of cramped postures and intellectual work. The muscles are to be used in such movements as will strengthen them enough to maintain the good posture gained and by their strength improve the great vital functions of the circulatory, respiratory, and digestive organs. No muscular work is undertaken for its immediate effect upon the muscles themselves, if it is not found, by looking behind this effect, that indirectly these vital functions are materially benefited. Thus follow first *movements for the back of the trunk*, to increase the strength of all the muscles of the back, principally in the thoracic region, to enable them to carry the shoulders and the chest in such a way as to give the necessary space for heart and lungs; then *movements for the front side*, principally to strengthen the abdominal walls, creating a firmer support for the abdominal viscera and making of them, so to speak, a natural apparatus for massage of these same viscera. Their increased strength and improved ability to function will cause more thoroughgoing kneading of the abdominal contents, which, in its turn, induces increased osmosis from the intestines, increased secretion from their glands, more rapid circulation, and a more effective peristalsis. The main object of the *movements for the sides* is of a similar nature, though different groups of muscles are brought to contraction or extension by them, and thus different regions may be specially affected. They will also increase the movability of the vertebræ upon each other, and affect both costal and diaphragmatic respiration; besides which they, according to some authorities, act as stimulants for the spinal nerves at their exit from the intervertebral foramina—a statement which appears to be based more on theoretical than experimental grounds, and therefore is not absolutely sure, though it appears probable.

If the allotted time is ample, it would be well to give another series of movements from these last families, of course of a different kind, but if so they ought to be separated from the preceding series by some movements which can give relief to the parts which have been in activity. For this purpose *rhythmical leg movements*, such as *marches and military evolutions*, are commonly employed. When the desired relief has been gained, these may be changed into the form of running, for the sake of training and strengthening the heart and lungs. If running is employed in this place it will, of course, be necessary to quiet the heart action and relieve the respiration, if it has become labored, before passing over to the next series of trunk movements.

If, on the other hand, one series of trunk movements must suffice, these marches will serve to give ease from the previous work, while the running forms a part of the *precipitant movements* proper. Under this term we embrace all such movements as demand a great expenditure of force in a short period of time, and which therefore are executed by great masses of muscles. Besides the running already mentioned, the different forms of jumping and vaulting are of this nature. Their physiological effect is the stimulation and strengthening of the circulatory and respiratory functions, which are charged with removing the great amount of waste materials formed in these movements and supplying the muscles with new nutrition. With these movements, the effect of which is the most general one of any of the groups spoken of, the day's order has reached its highest point of intensity, its climax, and it now rapidly descends toward complete rest through such movements as will quiet the heartbeat, accelerate the excretion of the results of the chemical combustions, and cool the body by increasing the secretion of the water from the lungs. It is the *respiratory exercises* which are most suitable for this purpose, and which should always end the day's work, as well as be employed whenever needed in the day's order; but they may well be preceded by *slow leg movements* on account of their derivative influence, and especially may these be very profitably employed in the form of balancing movements after such precipitant movements as jumping and vaulting, which are executed by one at the time, and after which each pupil may take such a movement by walking on the balancing beam in returning to his place in the rank.

In observing the list which is here recommended as a type suitable in a majority of cases, it will be found that there is a steady progression from milder to stronger movements within the day's order. But a steady progression must also take place from day to day or from week to week, and in no family must the progression advance to any extent without a corresponding progression within the other families, as this would be contrary to the rules of gymnastic totality and unity.

It is the hygienic basis of the day's order which we have endeavored briefly to sketch, because of the preeminent importance of gymnastics as a hygienic agent. So far as we know, the purely educational or psychological aims which may be reached by gymnastics are also best furthered by the same sequence and arrangement, though we cannot affirm this as positively as the hygienic benefits of the day's order, because of the few data collected by psychologists.

CHAPTER V.

EFFECT OF CERTAIN EXERCISES UPON THE PULSE-RATE.

OBJECT. The object of this chapter is, first, to present the results of observations, showing the effect of certain movements of the body on the action of the heart after jumping and running exercises. Second, to discuss briefly the reasons for placing precipitant, slow leg, and breathing exercises in the Swedish day's order where they are. Third, to bring up for discussion a few questions pertinent to the subject.

Why the Tests were made. Some years ago my attention was called to the reason for placing the jumping exercises after the motions for the "abdomen, fore part of the body, and alternate side movements." Baron Posse, in his "Chief Characteristics of the Swedish System," places the slow leg exercises before the jump, following it with breathing exercises. Jakob Bolin places precipitant work, his term for running and jumping, after the abdominal movements. The quieting of the action of the heart after violent exercises by slow leg motion and rhythmic breathing exercises seemed to be such a cardinal point in the Ling system, that I adopted the method and am still using it. As there is a unanimity of opinion among the advocates of the Ling system day's order, relative to the placing of such exercises, allow me to quote from one of the authorities, which quotation will agree in the main with the opinions expressed by other leaders. "The movements mentioned above, namely for the front, sides of the waist, and abdomen, following each other in the order named, are performed with gradually increasing force. By these movements the system is prepared for the next following. These are the more vigorous exercises of running and jumping. With these movements the culmination of the day's order is reached, after which the accelerated action of the heart must be normalized, and the body prepared for rest. This is accomplished by slow, measured, leg movements, accompanied by deep rhythmic breathing movements." *

It has often occurred to me that this arrangement of the approach to and departure from the precipitant work was like Mark Twain's description of the ascent of Mt. Vesuvius—long, gradual, moderate to the top; short and quick to the base. The first question, therefore, presents itself: If it is necessary to go through eight series of movements to prepare the heart for the strain of the jumping exercises, why are only two groups given to normalize its action? What objection can there be in the first series of these exercises arranged according to the Swedish day's order, to placing the running next to the abdominal work, when they can be so given in a second series, while in the more advanced arrangements they are sometimes placed in the middle of a group? These questions are asked because it is not clear to many teachers why this arrangement is so strictly adhered to. Another question arises: If the exercises involve a high

---
* Dr. Enebuske.

degree of heart exertion, but never exceed the danger limit, why are so few movements given to quiet the action of the heart? Why not give "in place rest," as well as slow leg exercises? If the precipitant work quickens the action of the heart and lungs, should we for the time attempt to normalize them? Is it not nature's method of meeting the condition? In any case of exertion would not rest be as judicious as a continuation of exercise? Is not the moment of complete relaxation between each of the movements of as much value in quieting the action of the heart as the exercises which follow?

The work being done at Yale University by Dr. Scripture, and at Harvard by Dr. Fitz, cannot but be of great service to the cause of physical education, while so high an authority as Dr. Ladd makes the statement that the relation between psychology and gymnastics is an intimate one. The teacher, whose duty it is to mold the bodies of men, and so the mind and feelings, should understand the elements of psychology, if, as has been stated, psychology is the mother of the science of education. In this research work I did not go out of my way to attack any system, nor to harbor any prejudice, but if a system is rational, and there is a scientific reason for everything adopted, then let it stand the test of investigation.

What the Tests were: With the aid of the kymograph, sphygmograph, time indicator, and smoked drum, these tests were made, with the assistance of members of the senior and junior classes of the Anderson Normal School of Gymnastics. Dr. Seaver took a number of the readings. Part of the tests were made with a Dudgeon sphygmograph. It is impossible to present all of the tracings, but attention is called to a few of the outlines, which are very similer to others secured by the same tests. Although the figures given are taken from one hundred and twenty persons, we have kept a record of a very much larger number, and it is found that when we increase the numbers there is not a great difference in the results. Of the one hundred and twenty, forty were experimented upon to show the effect of slow leg exercises and rhythmic breathing upon the action of the heart after running; forty more tried standing in "place rest" after the run, and the last forty took abdominal movements. In every case the normal pulse was read for thirty seconds. This was followed immediately by running in place, the person taking about seventy-five steps in half a minute, after which the pulse-rate was recorded for a period of thirty seconds, then followed four slow-stepping movements with each foot, and arm raising shoulder high to the side, accompanied by inspiration and lowered with expiration. The breathing movements were given four times, after which the pulse was read for the last time. We must bear in mind that during the half minute after the running exercise, while the pulse was being read, there was a period of rest; this might correspond to the moment of complete relaxation mentioned before. The second series of tests was given in much the same way, with this exception, that in place of the slow leg and breathing exercises, the pupil was required to hold the position of place rest thirty seconds, and in the last series the body was bent backward four to six times.

In the first series the total number of beats of the heart for forty persons was sixteen hundred and twenty-nine (1,629). After the run the pulse-rate went up to 2,227. It fell again after the leg work and breathing exercises to 1,668. In the second series of tests, the normal pulse was 1,648; after the run 2,228, and after place rest 1,646. The third series showed the normal pulse 1,699, after the run 2,326, and after abdominal work 1,703. The following table will perhaps make this plainer :

TEST.

1. Slow leg and breathing exercises,   1,629   2,227   1,668
2. Rest, or "In place rest,"   1,648   2,228   1,646
3. Abdominal work,   1,699   2,326   1,703

Another set of figures will show that in the case of the first forty who were experimented upon, the action of the heart was reduced below the normal in thirteen cases, above the normal in twenty cases, and was equal in seven cases. In the second test the action of the heart was below normal in seventeen, did not reach the normal in eighteen, and was equal in five. In the last test, the heart-beat was reduced below normal in nineteen, above normal in eighteen, and just the same in three, so that by looking at the following table we find that the abdominal work brought the heart down below the normal in the greatest number of cases, while the slow leg work and breathing show the least reduction. In the first test we find the greatest number who are above the normal after the so-called "normalizing exercises," while in the second and third they were the same. Finally, the slow leg and breathing exercises were given, and brought seven back to exactly normal condition. "In place rest" was given next, and abdominal work came last.

Test.	Below.	Above.	Normal.
1. Slow leg and breathing exercises,	13	20	7
2. Rest,	17	18	5
3. Abdominal work,	19	18	3

Fig. 1, standing normal, 1-2 m., 38.

Fig. 2, 30 seconds run, pulse-rate 75 for 1-2 m.

Fig. 3, after slow leg work and breathing exercises, pulse for 1-2 m., 39.

Fig. 4, after 1-2 m., "in place rest," pulse 39.

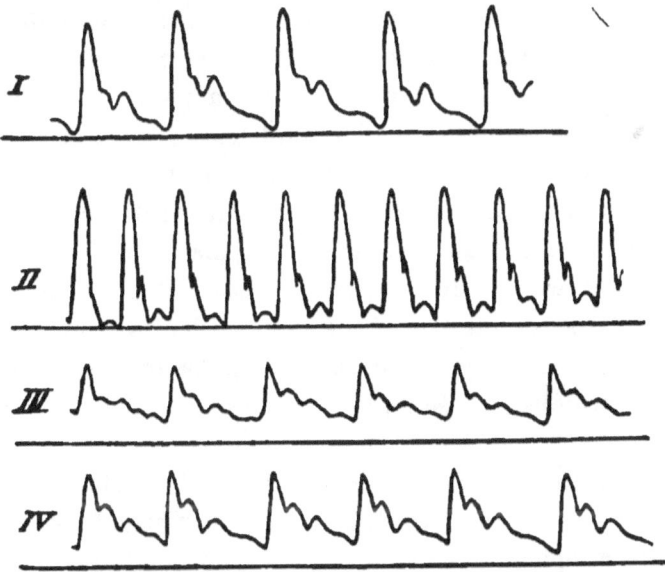

The tests recorded upon the revolving drum will not be given because they do not show quite so plainly as those by the Dudgeon sphygmograph. Fig. 1 shows the normal pulse, 38 beats for half a minute, person standing. This tracing is a fair sample of those taken from the normal pulse. Fig. 2 shows the pulse-rate after the patient has run in place for thirty seconds, the rate being 75. Fig. 3 gives the story of the pulse after thirty seconds of slow leg work and breathing exercises, the rate being 39, or one greater than normal. Fig. 4 shows the action of the pulse after thirty seconds in place rest. We notice by comparing Fig. 4 with Fig. 1 that it approaches nearer the normal than Fig. 3. In Fig. 4 the cardiac impulse is greater than in Fig. 3, the length of the tidal wave is about the same, there is some difference in the dicrotic wave, while the diastolic curve in Fig. 4 seems to be nearer that of Fig. 1 than does Fig. 3.

Conclusions. I do not wish to place myself on record as saying that these tests prove a point. They are interesting, however, and should lend some weight to these conclusions. Slow leg and breathing exercises tend to "normalize" the action of the heart after running, but this is also true of standing "in place rest," and abdominal work. But which is best? Pupils seem to prefer the first method if the choice is left to them. The tracings show that *rest* brings the pulse outline nearer the normal than do breathing exercises and slow leg work.

The statement has been made that "the Swedish system is rational, and there is a scientific reason for everything adopted." There is no doubt in my mind that the Swedish system in its theory approaches nearer perfection than any other; but there is some uncertainty among American teachers as to whether the statement should be made that the arrangement of the day's order is scientific. If this is true, and I have no reason for wishing it were not, the facts ought to be brought forward to prove it.

The attention of the reader is called to the reply to this chapter by Baron Posse. See *Posse Gymnasium Journal.*

CHAPTER VI.

STIMULUS, OR HOW TO AROUSE INTEREST.

G. STANLEY HALL says: "As teachers, we have to work more and more with interest. You cannot lay too much of the stress of educational work upon the will with children, but most of it must be done through interest. The value of your teaching is not the information you have to put into the mind, but the interest you have awakened. The mind is evolved out of heartiness. The characters of great men prove this. Whether in fiction or in prose, we are always coming up against the great fact that it is enthusiasm that governs the world."

President Eliot says: "The individual requires teaching in these days, and no teaching is good which does not awaken interest in the pupil."

To what qualities or methods is due the success which the best teachers achieve in stirring their pupils to attentiveness, to interest in their work, and, generally, to intellectual keenness and growth? This chapter is intended to draw particular attention to those qualities which are capable of being adopted or acquired, and are not merely natural gifts. "One great difficulty of my subject, every one will feel at once. It is this: that the power of stimulating pupils is so largely a matter of natural aptitude, a special form of genius, that it becomes not only very difficult to analyze, but it may even seem that the whole topic is at variance with the practical art of teaching. It is true, no doubt, that in all branches of teaching, the lively and attractive manner, quickness and adaptability and resource, insight into character and the speaker's instinctive sympathy with his audience, real personal interest, both in the studies and the students, force and variety and felicity of expression, wide and accurate knowledge, the power of seizing upon the telling points of a subject and presenting them suitably, apt and copious illustration, and, above all, a strong personality and high-mindedness of character— all these are most powerful stimulants to young natures brought under their influence, and all, or most of them, are hard, if not impossible, to give rules or codes of acquiring. They constitute, or they go far to constitute, the genius of the teacher."*

It is essential that the teacher shall have at his disposal a fund of illustrations, perhaps stories, and at times anecdotes. The first requisite in a teacher is that he shall be able to secure the attention of his class. Those who cannot do this have mistaken their vocation, they ought not to be teachers at all. Those who have the power of securing attention can usually do so with ease. It is an art that can be acquired by study.

My attention was called to the method adopted by a well-known Greek professor in one of our universities. It has been thought that there should exist between the teacher and the pupil an abyss or chasm, across which the scholar can never pass. The old-style teaching inculcated these ideas in the minds of our parents, and it

---
* Browning.

has been a difficult matter for them to change their views in the days of their advanced age. They are apt to think that the child should be taught as they were taught, that the methods which were used in disciplining them should be those of the present generation. They forget that the child is supposed to start from their shoulders, and is living in a more advanced age. The professor of Greek in one of our universities on one occasion startled the class by a very lively anecdote, which produced roars of laughter. It was a new idea to the boys that the instructor could be amusing, and to-day it is doubtful if there is a more popular professor on the faculty than this one, who, although willing to meet the boys on their own ground, to talk with them of their daily affairs and enter more into their lives, never permitted them to take liberties with him. This shows that a university professor can joke with students, be, to some extent, "one of the boys," and yet keep their respect.

An important question is, How can we stimulate attention, which is one of the requisites in producing interest? The obvious answer is, by making the lessons as interesting and amusing as possible. Interesting, of course, but how? Manner goes for something. The teacher can be easy, friendly, and familiar. Stiffness is a mistake. It has been said that the school-teacher must keep up his dignity. True, but it can be kept up in such a manner that the child is not repelled, but rather attracted. We do not expect a teacher of gymnastics to make a buffoon of himself, nor to allow the children to take liberties with him; but at the same time he can remember that the old saying, "Familiarity breeds contempt" is not in all cases true. A certain form of familiarity will breed contempt.

The teacher should pay much attention to little things, such as tend to stimulate, in the matter of education. The teacher's mind and sympathy should be constantly active on this point; he should cultivate fertility of resources in the minutiæ. As the Eaton grammar says, the nature of man is fond of novelty; and if this is so, how much more do we find it in the wide-awake, alert, healthy child!

All boys are fond of stories. They never tire of hearing of the deeds of heroes and of strong men. The man or woman who instructs boys should be familiar with the lives of the great and the strong men of history. Seldom has a class failed to pay strict attention when listening to the exploits of that well-known athlete, the father of his country. The story has been told many times how George Washington made a running broad jump of twenty-three feet, and held the world's record until a Brooklyn man finally jumped a few inches farther than he did. I should urge the teacher to read of the wrestling bouts of this well-known president. Speak of his height and stature. William Blaikie, in one of his lectures, used to mention the fact that George Washington was perfectly straight from the axilla to the hip, and that his wide waist was a sign of his enormous strength. What makes "Ivanhoe" interesting to many of its readers? The feats of Richard the First of England, whose mighty arm could wield the heavy sword. In Sir Walter Scott's "Talisman," boys read with great interest the test made by Richard the Lion-hearted, when, with his wonderful sword, he severed an iron mace measuring an inch in diameter; and they also wonder at the skill of Saladin, who, with his razor-edged scimitar cut in two the light silk handkerchief.

There is a book published called "The Wonders of Bodily Strength and Skill." The stories and histories taken from this book have frequently stimulated boys when they have become tired of the routine drill in the gymnasium. It is not necessary to go back to history to find the records of brave and strong men. We find them in our every-day life. Boys and girls are as much interested in the doings of the modern giant as they are in those of the ancient. Scholars can be stimulated to do what is right, to obey the laws of health, to be better children, if these stories are properly told. The reader should understand that these anecdotes are only incidents in the lesson. Often when the class is tired a short story will be most acceptable to them.

No one can successfully teach boys who does not know the nature of these young animals. This can be learned by carefully studying child-life. It is better to regulate our teaching by this knowledge than to work without it. For example, we know that all boys are fond of play; then make their work seem play to them. When a class of boys enter a gymnasium the first thing they do is to rush for some of the swinging apparatus; they turn their backs upon all the light appliances. Any experienced teacher of gymnastics has noticed this. What do we infer? That it is the wish of the boy to swing, to hang, or to go through some of the heavy gymnastic movements. He enjoys this work, it seems to be more in accord with his nature. Can we not, therefore, learn a lesson from this, and so arrange the gymnastic exercises that they shall be as attractive to the boy as the work which he takes of his own free will? I do not mean that the lessons in free gymnastics shall be discarded, because they are of great importance. The child should be daily drilled in the exercises that will tend to overcome the common physical defects. It soon becomes medicine to the boy, but it is essential, nevertheless, that every child should be trained in this way, and should not be allowed to feel that life is entirely free from restraint. Discipline is a good thing for a boy, it must be found in physical as well as in mental training. The gymnastic drill can be made very attractive to both boys and girls, if the teacher will use tact.

There are many things to be taken into consideration when we attempt to arouse interest. The teacher must, of course, be interested in the pupil; but this is not all. The pupil, on his side, must have his share of interest in the teacher. To arouse this feeling the master gains the confidence, the good-will, the respect of the boys. The limits of this chapter will not allow us to go into many of the details, but attention is called to the methods which have made some teachers interesting.

Personally, I have learned a great deal from two classes of instructors. In one case I worked because I feared them, and dreaded the results of not having a lesson. In the other case I had the utmost respect and love for the teacher, and was ashamed to fail. The question was raised by a minister in one of our churches once, when he said: "A person can be sent to heaven in two ways; he can either be allured by its attractions, or he can be frightened there by the horrors of the other place." So in teaching—a child will work, fearing punishment, or he will work because he loves the teacher. Of the two forms, of course, the latter is preferable.

Simplicity is very essential in any teacher. That instructor who can make his work so simple that it is understood by the dullard in the class will teach better than the one who selects the five or six bright ones and gives his attention to them. We are apt to make this mistake, and to teach the few rather than the many. One instructor claims that he watches the stupid boy in his class, and when he sees his face lighten up, knows that he has grasped the subject.

Another method of making the work interesting is to understand the subject thoroughly, to make a study of the methods of teaching, and to be a good gymnast. It has been said that it is not essential for the instructor in gymnastics to be a good exponent of his work, but if he can lead the class this will be sufficient. I have found, and others will bear me out in the statement, that many of our teachers fail because they are easily beaten by their own scholars in these gymnastic movements. I believe in what may be termed fancy gymnastics. They are the games and the sports which the young men in our gymnasia like. The teacher will arouse more interest and greater enthusiasm if he is able to take part in these sports than will the one whose knowledge is purely theoretical. Every young man who teaches gymnastics should become proficient in handling the heavy apparatus; what he does do he should do well. We admit, without dwelling at length upon the fact, that we have respect for those who know more than we do, who can do better work than we can, and that the reverse of this brings a reverse opinion. Therefore, in arousing or stimulating interest and keeping it up, I should say to the teacher of gymnastics, whether a man or a woman: Be proficient in your work, but remember, as Professor Richards has said, "The gymnastic work is not the ultimatum, but is the means to an end."

Interest. The teacher may learn something from Basedow, who taught his children by means of biscuits baked in the form of letters. The children were allowed to eat any letter which they could name.

Locke says: "Whatever children are deeply interested in they will never forget. Therefore I think it may be well to give the children something every day to remember, but something that is in itself worth remembering." A boy who cannot say his lessons may have an excellent memory for baseball or football, or may be able to describe accurately a trip he has made, a hunt upon which he has gone, or some other event associated with interest and pleasure. Do not, therefore, accuse your children of not having memories if they fail to repeat that which seems to them dry and monotonous.

A child will remember the foolish parts of a lesson and forget the wise parts. For example, it has been said that in reading the history of the life of a famous general, the boys never forgot the fact that his horse's tail was shot off in a certain battle, while the salient points of the history were not remembered twenty-four hours.

CHAPTER VII.

ATTENTION.

ATTENTION is so closely allied to interest that the author has thought best to write a short chapter upon this subject.

No teacher will succeed who has not the power of holding or maintaining the attention of the pupil. It is utterly impossible. Therefore it is necessary for the one who leads the class to, in some way, arouse and hold the attention of the child. Interest always begets attention; therefore, if you are not an adept at arousing attention, but have the faculty of creating interest, do the latter, because the former will follow. Condillac says: "The important point is to make the child comprehend what attention is." We do not believe, with Condillac, that this is the important point. It is not so much to teach the child to be attentive as the way to succeed in this. Do not explain theoretical conditions, because they amount to nothing; but interest the child. The teacher is sure of success, and instruction really begins, on the day that he has held the attention of his pupils for a certain number of minutes. It will be easily noticed that the scholars who have lost their interest, who are not sufficiently aroused to pay attention, will permit their eyes to wander. The time has now come for the teacher to act, and if the work that has been given to the child does not produce the desired result, a quick change of some kind should be made. That time is lost to the teacher and to the class when disorder reigns and the interest is lacking.

Attention, of course, requires the use of the will, and in this way we educate that important factor of the mind. We cannot attach too much importance to the subject. The history of the most brilliant scientific discoveries and of the great works of human art is, for the most part, but the recital of the efforts of the attention. Newton said that he discovered the laws of universal attraction by always thinking on the subject, or by paying attention. It is characteristic of a normal state of intelligence and, so to speak, the health of the spirit. That teacher who is not able to place her attention upon the subject is not, for the time being, in a healthy mental condition. The one who allows herself or her attention to be easily called away from the subject should investigate and ascertain the cause and then remove that cause.

Children are easily distracted, and distraction is the very opposite of attention. Therefore allow nothing to distract their attention. It is far better, in teaching children, that the room should be so arranged that nothing in the street or outside of the building will distract them. It is better to have the curtains raised from the bottom of the windows than to be lowered from the top. It is not a good plan to have in the room too many objects that will call their attention away from the lesson. It is unwise to allow a series of exercises to be carried on in one part of the room while the teacher is endeavoring to instruct a class in another. For example, we would not allow individual work of any character to go on while a class was being drilled in light gymnastics. The reason is obvious.

We should not expect or demand of a child real, absolute attention, and expect to maintain it for more than a few minutes. We might as well expect immobility on the part of a bird. Imposed attention, as mentioned by Payne, is a matter that requires some thought. The best plan will be to place a child in such a condition that nothing will excite distraction. Madame de Saussure has said: "Cause a calm to reign around the infant." On one occasion we requested our teacher to allow us to go to the orchard back of the school to study our lessons. We had a pleasant hour under the trees, but our lessons were not learned. Our attention was constantly called to what was going on in the trees, in the fields, or we were watching the boys in the lot below us, who were busy playing ball. So in teaching gymnastics. Do not allow anything to interfere with the lesson itself. The limit of a child's attention is soon exhausted. He will, moreover, apply it to what he is interested in.

Finally, in a general way, the attention of a child is weak, and there must be a resort to all sorts of stimulants which are healthy to arouse and keep it. Horace Grant has shown that beyond from five to ten minutes for young children and from thirty to forty-five for older pupils, the attention is wearied and intellectual effort comes to an end. We would not infer from this that a child can be taught but five minutes. It is well to compel them to pay strict attention to the lesson for a short time, then to allow them an interval of rest, such as would be given in the command, "In place, rest." They can be called to order and another exercise given, this to be followed by the interval of rest. It is not supposed, however, that the gymnastic lesson for a child will extend over a period of more than twenty to thirty minutes.

The child displays the whole of his power at the beginning of his task, but he is soon at the limit of his strength, and he needs to be occupied with something else. Be careful, then, to go gradually in your teaching. The lessons should be short at first and grow longer as the pupil's power of attention is developed. There should be a period of exercise, frequent commands of rest, and the interesting part of the work should be kept for the last of the lesson.

Avoid teaching to the child too early general truths, formulas, rules, or anything which repels him because he does not easily comprehend. One who has paid attention to the writings of Herbert Spencer cannot fail to be impressed with the emphasis which he places upon this idea. Avoid the parrot fashion. Do not cram a child's head with senseless maxims and axioms. He understands the reality. A child does not comprehend a joke for this reason. Elsewhere the attention of the reader will be called to the value of teaching children by the picture method, rather than the word. This is one of the quickest ways in which to hold the interest of a little child. We have found that it is a wise plan for the teacher to give what may be termed imitation work, which requires the constant attention of the child for a very short time. She may, for example, assume some posture and allow the child to copy that. This may be changed, and the child allowed to do as she does. Or the teacher may take a position, the child will study it for a minute; the teacher then resumes the fundamental standing position and asks the child to do as she did. We have held the attention of the child, and aroused interest. It is also well for the teacher to take some grotesque position or assume some awkward attitude, and allow the child to associate with this imitation work the element of fun or play.

The exterior signs which are characteristic of the attention of a child are rarely the same exterior signs which announce attention in the man or the adult. The man who thinks very frequently clasps the hands back of the body, walks up and down the room with the head bent forward. If he places his attention more directly upon the subject, he will frequently stand still, fold the arms in front, and drop the head still farther forward, or he may place the hand upon the forehead. We do not observe in a child similar signs of attention. It is impossible for a small boy or a small girl to think and remain immovable. The eyes will wander to the right or the left, some part of the body will move, and I know of one small boy who would fail in doing his sums in arithmetic if he were not permitted to chew the end of his lead pencil. In short, the child has need of movement, even when he is studying, and I should not allow the teacher to prevent all action if this is the nature of the little one. There is need of movement; therefore do not prevent it. No woman who has forgotten the nature of a child, or has forgotten what she used to do, should be permitted to teach boys and girls. Do not misunderstand me when I say that the child should be allowed to fidget while at work. There are exceptions to all rules, and I do not believe that the child should approach the movements of one who has St. Vitus' dance, but I would not shut off all movement from the thinking child.

The stimulants of attention, or the methods of buying interest, should be discussed. I believe there is not an educational institution of any importance in America that does not sanction the giving of premiums—in other words, the buying of attention and interest by gifts and honors. This is all right to a certain extent, but I do not believe that the interest of the class in gymnastics or of the individual should be purchased by the offer of a medal or reward; neither do I agree with that teacher who feels that she must compel the child, by threats or by the rod, to take the gymnastic movements or to excel in any bodily exercise. It is far better that the subject itself should be so presented by the teacher that the attention and interest will be aroused, and I know that a good teacher of gymnastics can do this without attempting to buy the interest of the scholar with promises of reward.

How to create interest is a study, and the success of any teacher will depend, to a great extent, upon this, what has been called by some, knack. Affection for the teacher will arouse interest and stimulate attention, and all teachers should at least have and hold the good-will of their pupils. Pleasure is a most powerful stimulant to effort, and the lesson that is pleasing will greatly stimulate the pupils. It has often been said that the Swedish system of gymnastics would fail in this country because it lacks the very essential element of interest. I believe that any good, energetic, wide-awake teacher can teach the Swedish system of gymnastics, and arouse as much interest as the teacher who gives her time entirely to the merits of the American plan. This was noticeable in the work of Miss Jennie Ireson, of Boston, who teaches in the schools of some of the adjoining cities the pure Swedish system, and in the public schools of another city what may be termed the American system. The little children were trained in the former method, and I have never seen happier, more interested children than I saw in her classes. The work was well done, well taught, while the children seemed to be inspired by the enthusiasm of the teacher.

We must bear in mind that if the class is not interested, or has not the power of placing its attention upon the work, there must be a cause. Let us, therefore, look for the cause and remove it, before attempting anything else. Simplicity, clearness, cleanness of exposition, will have a happy effect on the dispositions of the scholars in the class. We know that the tone of voice or attitude of the teacher will also arouse great interest in the work. These are but little things, but they will contribute greatly toward exciting the interest and holding the attention of those who learn a lesson.

I do not believe that we should always attempt to make everything agreeable and attractive. The children must understand that there is another side to this work, and that they must strive to overcome those obstacles which are not pleasing to them, in order that they may be better prepared to meet the world and the adverse criticisms which will be brought to bear upon them later in life. There are two sides to this question, and the child should know them both, but the successful teachers in the world have been those who understood the art of arousing interest and holding the attention.

Curiosity will always hold the attention of the class. The teacher who says to the pupils in her gymnastic class, "I want to show you a new exercise," will at once hold their attention, their curiosity. "Happy are those teachers who have to do with intelligences naturally curious, but especially happy are those who know how to excite curiosity and keep it active. For this purpose we must skilfully appeal to the tastes of a child and favor them, yet without overtaxing them."* "Eagerness to derive advantage from a taste is often a cause of our killing it." † We should not smother the curiosity of a child by satiating it too soon. We must bear in mind that the teacher of gymnastics does not come in such close contact with the children as do the teachers of the mental branches, with whom the child spends several hours a day. I should therefore advise the teacher of physical training to meet the children outside of the school, take them on walks, if necessary, allow them to visit the gymnasiums in the vicinity, and to give them once in a while practical talks on the care of the body.

---

* Payne.
† De Saussure.

In this way she will know the child better and will come into closer touch with the parents.

To arouse the attention give the children something new. Do not expect to succeed if you give a child the same work year after year. I know of no man who can equal in this respect Dr. Hitchcock of Amherst College, who could successfully teach the same dumb-bell drill for four years. It was not so much the arrangement of exercises that made this work popular, but the doctor himself. I have heard one Amherst man state that there was not another physician in America who could arouse and hold the interest of his pupils as could Dr. Hitchcock, whose name is synonymous with kindness and goodness. Avoid falling into a rut. Change the way of giving a command; suddenly stop an exercise and give one of another character. We may be violating, perhaps, some law laid down by the advocate of some other system of gymnastics, but I do not believe that any harm will result.

It is essential that the class should be kept good natured. When any faculty of a child is wearied, it is necessary to grant it some respite and make an appeal to other faculties. The mind of a child is just as eager for a change as that of an adult. Nothing is so difficult to listen to and to follow as the monotonous teaching of some of our instructors. Give to the class a few things, or only one thing, at a time, drill them a while upon this before passing to another. Children, as well as adults, will soon become dissatisfied with poor teaching, and they will discuss in their own little way a gymnastic exercise that is poorly taught and half learned. Mr.

Sully says he would be a foolish teacher who gave a child a number of disconnected things to do at a time, or who should insist on keeping his mind bent on the same subject for an indefinite period. I would say to the teacher, Do not become verbose, do not allow your thought to overflow its limits, do not talk too much. A child does not come to the gymnasium to be preached to for three quarters of its lesson.

Remember that action is essential in the education of a child. If talking or preaching or lecturing is to be done, it should be when the children are in the schoolrooms and seated. The story of the Esquimaux, as told by Miss Edgeworth, is interesting. Newly arrived in London, they had visited in one day all the monuments of the capital, under the conduct of a guide who was in too much of a hurry, and who was like too many teachers of gymnastics. On their return, when they were asked what they had seen, they did not know what to say. It was with difficulty that one of them, repeatedly urged to speak, finally aroused himself from his torpor and said, shaking his head, "Too much noise, too much smoke, too much houses, too much men, too much everything." According to M. Breal, "So far as possible, the teacher should keep his position, holding the class under his eyes and requiring that all eyes should be turned toward him. The instruction is not to begin until the children have taken the erect attitude. The lesson should not be continued until the class become impatient. As soon as inattention appears, the teacher stops. A means of reanimating the class, but a means which should not be abused, is to change the position of the class and begin a new exercise at the word of command. The pupils should always respond, if necessary, but they should not be accustomed to hear the explosive or the loud voice. Their ears soon become accustomed to the explosions of the voice, and then they are good for nothing."

Attention is stronger in the morning than in the afternoon, and it is stronger during the first hours of the session than later, although I have found that the first hour on Monday morning, or even Monday itself, is the hard part of the week. It is better to put on interesting work for Monday and for Friday, rather than to give it in the middle of the week. The teacher must take into account these differences, in order to meet them and to regulate the studies. Kant says: "Distractions ought never to be tolerated, at least in school, for they end by degenerating into habits. The finest talents are lost in a man who is subject to distractions. Inattentive children only half hear, reply wholly at random, and do not know what they read." Cannot this rule be just as readily applied to some of our teachers of gymnastics as to children?

CHAPTER VIII.

DISCIPLINE, OR SCHOOL GOVERNMENT.

It has been said that the disciplinarian, as the teacher, is born and not made. There is truth in the statement, but it does not follow that the disciplinarian cannot be made. There are rules formulated that will be of service to any teacher. The man or woman fortunate enough to be included in the class of those who are born teachers does not depend so much on these laws, although unconsciously applying them. On the other hand, the unfortunate who belongs to the class of those who are not born teachers should know the rules that are of the greatest importance in teaching.

Discipline should be enforced in any class. In the gymnasium it is almost of vital importance that the teacher have order. Much of the success of the leader depends upon good ruling. One may be called upon to give instruction to a class of small boys. To know something of the nature of this small American, visit the gymnasium some day and study him. Full of life, energy, and vitality, it is almost impossible to keep him within bounds. He will disobey commands without meaning to do so, because of the surplus of animal life, causing the inexperienced teacher, who is apt to lay all this trouble to the natural depravity of boys, to lose her temper and scold. It will require patience and tact to handle a class of boys. The teacher should understand them—the men, remembering that they were once boys, and the women, that they at some time had small brothers. The teacher should be wide-awake, alert, seeing everything, forgetting self, and very positive.

As a rule, we can lay disorder, confusion, irregularity, and accidents to the teacher, and not to the pupil. Even if it is not the fault of the teacher, it will reflect back upon the management of the gymnasium. The small boy is apt to break away—in other words, to unconsciously violate the rules. One of the best plans of circumventing this is to remove temptation from him. The temptation may be in this form: The boy is permitted to go to the gymnasium before the allotted time for the lesson, in which case there is neither teacher nor assistant to supervise. He can then use any piece of apparatus he wishes. Several may struggle for the bar or the rings, and it not infrequently happens that a child is hurt at this time. Again, instructors are careless about leaving the apparatus so that it can be easily handled by the boys. All rings, bars, ropes, and poles should be either removed or pulled up. The ticks should be packed away in one corner, and everything that is within the reach of the members of the class should be disposed of or fastened, with the exception of the light apparatus and the chest weights. If the boys cannot use the heavy appliances they will go for the light. They find pleasure in pulling at the chest weights, letting the carriages drop, in which case they are frequently broken or cracked; or they will remove the dumb bells from the racks and skate around the room on them.

DISCIPLINE, OR SCHOOL GOVERNMENT.

There should be a certain number of rules made, these rules to apply to all classes in the gymnasium; but a rule is worse than useless if it is not enforced. It is well to have but a few of these regulations, but there must be one rule to govern these, namely, enforce them. There may, some day, come to the class the sons or the daughters of the principal, trustee, or some professor in your school. They are in their own, and too often in their parents' minds, privileged. They think, because their father is at the head of the school, or the mother is employed as a teacher, that they are entitled to do a little more than the others. Consequently, they are hard to manage. If that boy violates a rule his neighbor can do the same. Because the first lad is backed up by influence, he is not therefore entitled to privileges that should not be extended to others.

A teacher will often be called upon to deal with the parents, in which case she should use patience, tact, and, above all, keep her temper. The boy who is not in the habit of obeying at home will not do so at school. The teacher must be prepared to deal with this specimen. No instructor can successfully cope with the members of such a class unless she has made a study of boys, understands their nature, has a great deal of patience, and is able to meet them and to deal with them as she should.

"Children rarely love those who spoil them, and they never trust them. Their keen young sense detects the false note in the character, and draws its own conclusions, which are very generally just." Herbert Spencer says: "Let the history of your school work typify a little the history of our political rule—at the outset autocratic control where control is needful; by and by an incipient constitutionalism, in which the liberty of the subject gains some express recognition; successive extensions of this liberty of the subject, gradually ending in paternal abdication." I may also add, in the abdication of the teacher. "If that child is unhappy who has none of his rights respected, equally wretched is the little despot who has more than his own rights—who has never been taught to respect the rights of others, and whose only conception of life and living is that it is an absolute monarchy, of which he is the sole ruler." The teacher must be prepared to meet just such a child. It may be of assistance to the young teacher to call to mind some case in which she has the power to control either boys or girls. It may be one, or it may be more. Is this control due to fear, or to love? If it is possible for a teacher to manage one, it will also be possible for her to manage many.

The teacher must not be a coward. Unfortunately, too many of our instructors are timid. They are either afraid to hurt the feelings of a scholar, or they fear the consequences if they interfere with the children of influential parents. As a teacher or a director, do not be afraid to assert your own rights. There is always some scholar in your class of whom you will stand somewhat in awe. It may be because he is disagreeable; it may be because he has a little of the bull-dog element about him; it may be that you can get along better by letting him alone. He will very soon find this out, and the other boys will notice it. The matter will be discussed; it will later on cause trouble in the school. The first case, therefore, will decide a great deal for the new teacher. This must be treated quickly and firmly. Always hear the boy's side of the story, if there is any doubt about his wrong-doing. Do not be too quick and hasty. Do not punish a child without first permitting him to say why he did this or to give some reason, unless you know that his act was a strict violation of the rules. Under no conditions lose your temper. If you do, do not attempt to punish the boy at that time. The members of classes take delight in "rattling" the teacher. It is a pleasure to boys to do this. They will try in every way, they will test the teacher, or, as Professor Parker says, "they will puncture your moral anatomy with pins, if they find that there is an opportunity." A teacher can establish a reputation after the very first command is given to a class. For example, she directs them to fall in in single file. They take their places. One boy is late; he dilly-dallies, evidently heard the command, but did not obey it. This is the time for the teacher to act. She promptly calls this young man to account, and in such a way that it leaves no doubt in his mind or in the minds of the class about her intentions. The voice need not be entirely devoid of kindness, but it must be positive. When the teacher says to the boys, "I want you to do so and so," that must settle the question.

There is a custom adopted by some teachers of calling to the platform the scholars who are out of order. Doing this punishes the honest ones, while the dishonest ones go free. Those who are truthful receive punishment as a reward; those who lie are enabled to go free because of their falsehood. Sending from the room is a method of punishment that should not be used a great deal, although sending a boy home from the gymnasium will frequently bring good results. The child who is sent from the gymnasium back to the classroom may find time to make up some study, to loiter in the halls, or to play, and will very likely present his own case to his teacher, who will not have the time or inclination to hear the instructor's side of the story. Again, every boy who is sent from the gymnasium to the regular teacher carries additional care to her. The instructor in gymnastics should assume all this responsibility, and should be liable for the government of her own classes. The principal of one school was in the habit of saying to his gymnastic director, "If your pupils are out of order, send them at once to their classrooms, and the regular teacher will remain with them after school." This was tried a few times, until the gymnastic instructor ascertained that he was creating a strong feeling against him, because he compelled other teachers to remain after school to punish those who did wrong in the gymnasium. If you cannot deal with or punish your own pupils, do not teach gymnastics.

It is not necessary in this chapter to discuss the question of corporal punishment. In my own experience, I have never had to "whip." The relations between myself and pupils have never called for blows.

There is a subject that it will be well to discuss under this heading, namely, sarcasm. The real significance of this strong, harsh Greek term is to tear the flesh, like dogs. Caroline B. Le Row says: "By easy and natural transfer, this becomes identified with intellectual and verbal laceration of a corresponding character. It is the expression of contempt, anger, jealousy, bitterness, disappointment, of malice, hardness, and all uncharitableness, in language more or less disguised, in a form of words which in letter may not offend, but which in spirit are as objectionable as they can be made. The relation of the teacher to the pupil is that of youth depending upon maturity, weakness upon strength, awkwardness upon skill, inexperience upon expertness, ignorance upon wisdom. Can anything be more revolting than for this superiority of age and strength and experience to browbeat youth, weakness, and ignorance?" A sarcastic teacher can never be a teacher in the true sense of the word. She lacks that element which is found in every great instructor in the world, kindness; and although the scholars may learn and make some progress, nevertheless there is between the teacher and the pupil a barrier that will never be entirely broken down. The teacher is heartily disliked by the scholars, who fear her bitter tongue. There are times when certain forms of sarcasm can be used. There is in every class a mean boy. To him, it may be that this verbal laceration of the flesh will bring good results. But, as a rule, avoid sarcasm, so far as it is possible. It is the weapon used more by the young teacher. The student from college, who hears a great deal of this among his fellow students, is apt to use the same weapon when he takes charge of a school. Parents are frequently too sarcastic when correcting their children. It is neither wise nor safe. Corporal punishment is less obnoxious than cutting words and sarcasm. Bodily pain is very soon forgotten, but shaming a person hurts the soul, and is never forgotten.

A few years ago a German newspaper contained the statement that a boy had committed suicide because his teacher called him a thief. He took an apple that belonged to another boy. Jean Paul Richter, who understood the child, said: "What is to be followed as a rule of prudence, yea, of justice, toward grown-up people, should be much more observed toward children. One should never say, for instance, 'You are a liar,' or even, 'You are a bad boy,' instead of, 'You have told an untruth,' or 'You have done wrong.'" Children usually feel when they have committed a fault without being told, and certainly they do not wish to have it, as the boys say, "ground in." If it is necessary to say something, the wrong should not be made greater than it is. Never brand a culprit with an opprobrious name. The teacher should be very careful about making remarks that will hurt the feelings of pupils. Edward Eggleston says: "The test of a teacher is efficiency, not only in teaching, but in her dealings with others; not as showing that she is able to make an examination, but the final result she can produce in the character of those who come from under her hand. This efficiency is not of the sort that can be counted upon always to work an increase of salary, but the ability to leave a lasting mark on the mind and character of the pupil. It is an unmistakable sign of a real teacher, and the source of this power lies, not in the teacher's knowledge, but deeper, in the fiber of his character."

One of the most important objects of school discipline

is the formation of the habit of self-control. The power to govern well is an essential quality of every successful teacher. The opinions of the scholars themselves should be used, so far as possible, as an aid to the teacher. A boy is often influenced by the judgment of his fellows more than by the decisions of the teacher. There are, in every school, college, or university, leaders in right-doing, and ring-leaders in wrong-doing. The teacher should captivate one set, and the capture of the others will assist in bringing good government. Eternal vigilance is the price of order in the schoolroom. The teacher should have an eye like a hawk, and be quick to detect noise. "Disorder is the sure sequel of the teacher's failure in sight or hearing; but even with the senses good there may be absent the watchful employment of them. This is, in itself, a natural incapacity for the work of teaching. A teacher must not merely be sensitive to incipient disorder; he must read the result of his teaching in the eyes of his pupils. By organization and arrangement, the occasions of disorder are avoided. The reasons for repressions and discipline should, so far as possible, be made intelligible to those concerned, and should be made referable solely to the general good." The teacher will be able, in many cases, to anticipate disorder. If, from experience, she knows that certain movements are attended with confusion, she can ward off the difficulty. She should encourage truth by rewarding full and frank confessions with a remission of penalties, so far as consistent. Severity is one of the chief causes of deceit. Prevention is better than punishment. Children should be trained to a general habit of prompt obedience in minor matters.

Penalties and punishments must be certain, and must seem to be the natural consequence of wrong action. Strong terms of reproof should be sparing, in order to be effective. Still more sparing ought to be the terms of anger. Do not make cast-iron rules, with unchangeable penalties. There can be no government where there is no punishment. Swett says: "The chief means of preventing the necessity of punishment are active and pleasant employment, the personal influence of the teacher, the public opinion of the scholars. The punishment must be varied according to the temperament of the child. A frown will act on one, separation from companions on another, neglect and coldness on a third, public reprimand on a fourth." If the teacher has a case that calls for severe punishment, it is better for her to consult the parents before taking action.

Discipline. M. Buisson says: "There should never be irony, never contradictions and paradoxes, never anything which exalts the teacher at the expense of the pupil; much indulgence and no trace of weakness; nothing exciting or brusque; an inflexible firmness and a paternal gentleness; inexhaustible simplicity in all things; finally, a constant effort, which becomes insensible in the course of time, to come down to his plane, to understand him, to sustain him, to love him."

Obedience is one of the important things for a child's character. It is an important agent in the development of a child, and will result from good teaching. Many of our instructors are fatigued, not by the teaching itself, but by the enforcing of discipline.

"The punishment of the child may be physical or it

may be moral; moral where we act on the child's natural desire for love and affection, physical when we punish him by denying him what he wants or giving him what he does not desire."

Contempt is a strong punishment. Kant says: "The powers of the mind are best cultivated when we do things for ourselves. The duties of a child toward himself are cleanliness, purity, sobriety, and the most important safeguard of all is the possession of a certain self-respect which he values beyond everything else." The teacher herself can learn from this quotation. There is truth in the maxim that the teacher who has not great respect for herself will not receive it from others.

A characteristic of the school of humanists, which included Locke, Rabelais, Basedow, and others, is their preference of kindness to severity, and their condemnation of the cruelty and harshness which disfigured the schools of the Middle Ages. They believed that the principal method of compelling the attention of children and inducing them to learn with pleasure was preferable to pain. Locke says: "The usual lazy and short way, by chastisement and the rod, which is the only instrument of government that teachers generally know or ever think of, is the most unfit of any to be used in education. I cannot think that any correction is useful to a child where the shame of suffering for having done amiss does not work upon him more than the pain. Such a sort of slavish discipline makes a slavish temper. Beating them, and all other sorts of slavish and corporal punishments, are not a discipline fit to be used in the education of those we would have wise, good, and ingenuous men, therefore very rarely to be applied, and that only in great occasions and cases of extremity."

If a child tells a lie, he should be treated with contempt. Let him know that he will not be believed in the future and that you have lost your faith and confidence in him. The child punished when he misbehaves and rewarded when he does well acts, not for the good itself, but for the reward which he may receive.

Montaigne discountenanced severe discipline, and especially corporal chastisement. He says: "This education must be regulated by strict mildness, not as it is now. Instead of tempting children to the letters, nothing is shown them but what is terrifying and cruel. Put aside violence and force. There is nothing, in my mind, which so degrades and stupefies a naturally fine and noble disposition. What a way of awakening in the tender and timorous mind of children an aptitude for learning, to lead them to it with a whip in hand! Unrighteous and hurtful system!"

MISTAKES IN TEACHING.

Many of the following are from different authors:

It is a mistake to confound giving information or evidence with tale-bearing. Wise teachers never seek occasion for making an investigation of a petty nature.

It is a mistake to try to teach without good order.

It is a mistake to confound securing order with maintaining order.

It is a mistake to try to startle a class into being orderly.

It is a mistake to call for order in general terms, however quietly it may be done.

It is a mistake to scold an entire class for the fault of one.

It is a mistake to call to the platform all who have been out of order.

It is a mistake to be demonstrative in maintaining discipline. One teacher secures the silent coöperation by the natural laws of good organization, careful forethought, and by a quiet self-control.

It is a mistake to be variable in discipline. Confidence is necessary on the part of both teacher and pupils. A threat implies that the teacher does not trust the pupils, and prevents the class from having sympathy with her. The teacher should anticipate the movements that cause trouble, and forewarn the class. The boy who does behind the teacher's back what he will not do to her face is a coward.

It is a mistake to make too many rules. Some teachers make so many that they cannot remember them themselves. Their pupils forget them, too, and violate them without intending any wrong.

It is a mistake to make rules that are not enforced. The breaking of a rule should be considered a serious offense. Pupils who are old enough should have reasons for rules explained to them, so far as it enables them to see their justness. Indeed, judicious teachers may allow their scholars to assist them in framing rules.

It is a mistake to teach too much in a single lesson.

The teacher cannot furnish rules for every emergency, but can inculcate principles to be applied when the emergency arises.

Physical exercises, practiced frequently, save time by

improving the discipline and preventing irritation to both teacher and pupil.

It is a mistake to make promises and not keep them.

It is a mistake to say that you will do, and then do not.

It is a mistake to judge before hearing. Hold an angry tongue, and think before speaking.

It is a mistake to give gymnasium work as punishment.

It is a mistake to allow the class to be idle.

It is a mistake to pay attention to the bright scholars in the class, and neglect the stupid ones.

It is a mistake to talk too much.

It is a mistake to be too indefinite in teaching.

The teacher should not stand in awe of her pupils. She should never sanction tale-bearing.

It is a mistake for the teacher not to keep a record of what she is to give.

It is a mistake to regard knowledge as of greater importance than the child.

It is a mistake not to let children know that success costs something.

It is a mistake to confound fame with reputation.

It is a mistake to complain or grumble too much. If there is one teacher who, more than any other, is certain to be disliked by pupils, parents, trustees, it is the inveterate grumbler. She would dislike herself if she had the honor of her own acquaintance. She does not know how tiresome this habit becomes. No teacher who scolds a class or grumbles can ever have the sympathy of her pupils, and without it she can never control them or secure their best efforts in their school-work. She who recognizes, appreciates, and judiciously commends the feeblest efforts of her pupils will be certain, by this means, to induce greater zeal and earnestness.

RELATIONS OF THE TEACHER TO THE PARENT.

It is a mistake to show temper in dealing with a parent.

It is a mistake not to hear the parent's side of the story.

It is a mistake to express opinions too freely where a child has done wrong.

It is a mistake to dispute with an angry parent before the class or the scholar.

It is a mistake to make spiteful remarks before the class about the notes received from parents.

It is a mistake to make a remark that will insinuate that the parents are careless in the rearing of their children.

It is a mistake to neglect opportunities for arousing the active coöperation of parents in your work.

It is a mistake to let any insinuation made about you by parents go unanswered.

It is a mistake to discuss school affairs too freely with parents. Remember that the interest of the parents in the school is in proportion to the love they have for their children.

Rousseau, in his advice to teachers, says: "Teach a little, and that little well." Pestalozzi says: "I will put the education of the child into the hands of the mothers; I will transplant it from the school to the house. But how can a mother teach what she does not understand?" This rule will apply well to the introduction of home gymnastics. The teacher should endeavor to arouse in the parents enough interest in the work to have them require the children to do the exercises morning and night, just as they would care for the hair, the hands, or the teeth. But parents do not know the exercises; they think they have done their whole duty by the children when in peremptory language they command them to "stand up straight" or to "hold the head up." It is an important principle in education that children should not be educated for their present condition, but for the future of the human race; this education can be furthered by the teaching which a child will receive from the father and the mother. That parent who places the entire responsibility for the physical, mental, and moral education of children upon teachers is making a serious mistake.

CHAPTER IX.

ANALYSIS.—SYNTHESIS.—REFLEX ACTS.

THERE are two related methods of teaching, known as the analytic and the synthetic. In the former method analysis is used. By this term is meant the breaking up or loosening of the parts that make the whole—the dissecting, separating, or dissolving of the elements. Analysis can be applied to any complex or any compound exercise.

The analytic method is valuable, and should be used by teachers of gymnastics. G. Stanley Hall is of the opinion that the day of the analytic school is past, and that in the future we shall deal more with synthesis. It has been found, nevertheless, that analysis of gymnastic exercises will assist teachers. Illustration: Place in the hands of a child a watch; he is not satisfied until he has seen the "wheels go 'round." Nor is this sufficient; he is anxious to take the watch apart to see how it is made. When this is done, the child finds the various parts of the mechanism; he has to some extent analyzed the watch. An instructor when teaching writing divides the letters into straight and curved lines. The child is then drilled upon the parts. But before he can put them together or rearrange the elements, he has been taught to make them. Reading is taught by words, words by letters or sounds. Thus we go from the whole to the part. In grammar, the sentence is subdivided into its parts, its parts are separated into smaller divisions, which are finally reduced to the individual portions or parts of speech. In gymnastics, take, for an illustration, this exercise, which consists of the following parts of the gymnastic alphabet: Turning the head to the left, swinging the wand to the front, stepping the right foot to the right. This is the exercise as a whole, and is seen in the illustration (Fig. 5). The parts are: first, turning the head to the left; second, swinging the wand to the front; third, stepping the right foot to the right. As an exercise the movements cannot be well joined until they have been thoroughly learned by the pupil, therefore the teacher should reduce the posture, as a whole, to its simplest movements, and teach them. This may be called the analytic method.

In the synthetic method of gymnastics, we begin with the parts, or the movements of the alphabet, and proceed to the complete exercise, or the whole. At times the two methods are so nearly alike that they are confusing. In beginning with analysis we end with synthesis, and in beginning with synthesis we end with analysis. To illustrate. The teacher has in mind an exercise that may be called compound; the pupils do not know what this is. The teacher will explain each part of the drill, direct the scholars to take them, and then, by putting all together, make a complete whole. As in the illustration, the instructor will first drill the class in the stepping motion until it is mastered, then the arm movements, finally the head exercise. This may be termed synthesis.

The gymnastic instructor who has time to read the various works on methods of teaching will be interested in the inductive and deductive methods of teaching. As we shall not use these terms, we shall not take the space to describe them or to dwell at length upon their meaning.

Automatic Movements and Reflex Action. The terms automatic and reflex action will be so often used that it is necessary to explain their meanings here. The authorities on physiology and psychology agree that the terms overlap each other to such a degree that they are almost synonymous. There is a slight difference between the terms, but it is so slight that we shall not make a distinction in this work.

If the mind were occupied with every movement we make, we could do but one thing at a time. If one started out for a walk he would be able to think of nothing but how to take the steps; he could therefore neither talk nor observe. If one tried to take notes at a lecture he could do nothing but pay attention to the writing, if this was in charge of the mind itself. Women can both sew and talk at the same time, but if it happens that there is a knot in the thread, they will cease talking for a brief period until the knot is untied.

Actions which are repeated many times are referred back to a nerve or spinal center, so that the mind itself can be used for other duties. In walking, we are unconscious that we move or act, because the walking is looked out for by this nerve center. If we have learned to walk badly, the center which controls this movement does not worry over this, but it sees that the movement is executed as it has been learned. Hence the necessity of doing well whatever we do. The instructor in gymnastics should make many of her gymnastic movements automatic, in order that the mind may be given to the control or the teaching of the class. Every person who has attempted to teach an exercise that has not been well learned knows that, by dividing the attention between the movements which are poorly executed and the instruction of the class, both will suffer. By referring to any good work on physiology, the teacher will be able to study and learn more of these two terms.

CHAPTER X.

WHY DO WE TEACH?—WHO SHALL TEACH?

LET us spend a few minutes upon the first question, Why do we teach gymnastics? The answer may be given in a few words: because the needs of the pupil demand it. We are then confronted with another question, What are these needs? They are: (1) better health; (2) greater strength of body, properly distributed; (3) better physiques; (4) grace of movement; (5) self-control; (6) self-reliance; (7) nerve and brain training; (8) memory exercises; (9) mental rest; (10) recreation. The teacher will find, by referring to the German, Swedish, and Delsarte systems, that each claims the same results. Let us take time briefly to consider some of these results.

Better health. That all persons wish to be healthy is a fact. That all persons are not healthy is a fact. Of the two sexes, more women are sickly than men, more doctors make good incomes by treating women than by treating men. There is a reason for this. Women have neither the health nor the strength that men have, and yet no one will deny that they are called on to fulfill duties that require both. That the health is improved by a proper course in gymnastic drill is true.

Greater strength. People are apt to confound health and strength. The terms are not synonymous. The strength of the body is not proportionately distributed. A man may have enormous arms and chest, powerful legs, and a weak waist. The strength of the person may be compared to a chain. If one link is defective, the whole chain is weak. So in the body—unless the parts are so strengthened that one will assist the other, the strength is not what it might be. A man may have great strength but poor health.

It is astonishing that so many of our giants die quickly. Men who make their living by lifting heavy weights, wrestling, and boxing, go down suddenly, many of them dying of lung trouble. We understand that dissipation has much to do with their sudden demise. The statement is made to show that the enormous strengh which these men acquire does not indicate perfect health.

Better physiques. We admit that the physique is improved by physical training, but we have not yet reached that position in our science or art where we can change it to any great extent, unless the training begins with the child and is permanently continued. The boy is apt to be like one of the parents. If he inherits from the mother a slender, slight physique, he is liable to possess it always. The round-shouldered youth, or one with drooping head, does not often get rid of these defects. Many of our teachers of physical training do not show the results of their gymnastic drill in their personal appearance.

The point now arises, Does any method of physical training that is advocated to-day produce a perfect physique? The answer is, No. It does not follow, however, that the body is not bettered by a system of rational gymnastics. If the bone growth is established, it will be well-nigh impossible to straighten the spine, arch the chest, and overcome some of the physical defects. Yet it is true that the muscular system is invigorated, the action of the heart strengthened, the capacity of the lungs increased, the muscular coats of the arteries and veins improved, and the whole physical condition bettered; but there is not that change in the form that we look and hope for.

Grace of movement. All systems claim this to be a resultant. If one could be graceful by wishing, he would ask it. A person can acquire muscular control, which is the same as grace, by paying attention to rational physical training. This does not mean entirely light work or heavy work, but a wise combination of the two. Some of the most graceful men are jugglers. It is seldom that we meet a tumbler who is not easy in his movements, while many of the bar men exhibit this grace.

Self-control and self-reliance. While these are not the same, yet they are interlaced. One who can control himself to any great degree, who never shows emotion, who is calm and self-contained in the face of danger, who curbs his temper, is not cast down by grief, checks an angry word—in short, who can manage himself— exhibits self-control. All emotion is expressed by muscular movement, muscular movement is controlled by the will. The control of the muscles by the will is physical training of a certain order, it is physical education of the highest sense. It may be said that "man has never taken gymnastics in his life yet he never loses his self-control." True, but he has practiced this special form of physical education.

Self-control is the mastery over the restless muscles of the body. It is essential in the teacher. She is called upon every hour of the day to hold herself in check.

What is the loss of self-control? Visible emotion. How do we express any emotion but by muscular movement? Anger, sadness, joy, fear, jealousy are all shown in this way. When we are suddenly confronted with unpleasant news our muscles, like wild horses, at once slip from our control and we show by the face, if in no other way, that we are affected.

The teacher, lawyer, minister, or public speaker should rely upon himself, should have confidence in his own ability, should be free from mannerisms, affectations, should have a good presence, strong voice, and "staying qualities."

These are some of the results of physical training. Fortunate it is for us that the results of such an education are not only great strength, perfect health, and a fine physique.

The author quotes from Prof. Eugene L. Richards, the director of the Yale Gymnasium: "The effect of exercise on the character is felt most of all on the will. This is very natural, for in all muscular exercise a certain amount of resistance has to be overcome, and the power which acts through the muscles to overcome this resistance is will power. Development of muscular strength is, therefore, to a certain extent development of will. It becomes development of the highest kind of will, that of self-mastery, when to take exercise a man resolutely overcomes the distaste for it."

Mental rest and recreation. That certain forms of gymnastics will rest the brain and that children and adults find recreation in games and contests is true, but the gymnastics should be of the kind that do not require mental effort if the pupils are mentally fatigued. Do not give memory exercises to persons who have for some time used the brain. They can take simple movements and imitation work, and find pleasure in them too. A class undergoing a long examination will do better work if required to take a few arm and leg motions when the time is half over. This drill rests the brain. (See chapter on Swedish day's order.)

Memory exercises. There are a number of drills that are interesting to pupils which may be termed memory exercises. They consist of exercises not shown but explained. For example, the teacher describes a simple exercise and requests the pupils to execute it for her. They have not seen it but they will, according to their idea of what is meant, go through certain motions.

The child thinks and acts according to the muscular translation of its thoughts, and draws with its little body the picture that is in its mind. If writing or drawing is of value as a means of education so will gymnastics be if taught in this manner.

Example of a lesson in memory work. The teacher says: "On the count one raise the arms to the front, on the count two swing them out, on the count three slap them over the head, on the count four lower them to the side, *ready*, BEGIN."

Again the teacher may bring into action one or more sets of muscles or nerves in this way. The first exercise may be a head bending to the right, the second a combination of the head and arm movement, while the third will be the addition of a leg motion. All movements in the same direction are easier than those in different directions.

Another form of teaching will be imitation, which differs from the memory method. Here there are no commands, as the child is obliged to look at the teacher, then imitate her. The instructor begins by taking some simple movement, which the child at once imitates. This plan will teach a child to observe.

In drawing, good results depend upon the attention which a child pays to detail, so in imitation work the pupil is taught to look carefully and to place its own body in a similar position.

Scholars will soon learn to make changes very rapidly. An eminent psychologist favored this plan of teaching.

Another plan often used is for the teacher to read verses and let the children imitate the person or things represented in the poem.

Round work. This consists in giving a drill in gymnastics after the plan of singing a round, like "Three Blind Mice."

There may be four or more rows of scholars, the first of which begins with a leg exercise. After having taken the movement eight times the second row will begin, and so on. After the first row has finished its leg work it will take a drill for the neck, then for the arms and shoulders, going through a regular lesson.

The best plan is for the teacher to give the lesson as a whole, that the pupils may become familiar with the exercises, then to start the first row in the manner named.

Who should teach gymnastics? The answer is, Only that one who is competent. Again, Who is competent? A good gymnast? No. A person who is remarkably graceful? No. Neither strength, physique, nor great personal beauty makes one competent to teach gymnastics. It is the one who knows *how* to teach. The physique may be poor, both health and strength may be lacking, but there will be left the faculty of imparting knowledge to others. There must be the power and example of enthusiasm, which makes a natural leader. No one can teach gymnastics who is not *in some way* a good representative of the work. It is necessary to understand the theory and practice of gymnastics and to have mastered bodily exercises.

CHAPTER XI.

OUTLINE LESSONS ON PARTS OF THE BODY.

The outline lessons on the parts of the human body are intended to assist the teacher, both in speaking and teaching. The young men or women who are engaged as instructors in normal schools should not only be able to give instructions in gymnastics, but they should be able to prepare for their teachers short talks upon the reasons why exercises are given. There will not be, in this book, sufficient space to dwell at length upon the various portions of the body, but the teacher who is anxious to know more of this work can, by referring to Public School Syllabus,* prepare her talks, basing them upon the outlines found under the different headings. The author has dwelt at length upon the arms, the shoulders, and the thorax. The articles on the neck and legs can be filled out by the teachers themselves. Such a plan as this would be called the "skeleton" of a lecture.

OUTLINES OF LESSONS ON PARTS OF THE HUMAN BODY.

THE HEAD.

Subject: Head and neck.
Definition.

---
*"Syllabus of Gymnastics," Anderson.

OUTLINE LESSONS ON PARTS OF THE BODY. 123

Normal position. (See position of a soldier, page 183.)
Defects :
   (1) Drooping.
   (2) Carried on one side.
   (3) Chin elevated or protruding.
   (4) Wry neck.
Results of these defects on the shoulders and thorax.
Treatment :
   Drooping head. Cause. Bending, turning, forcing, rolling.
   Head carried on one side. Cause. Bending, turning.
   Elevated chin. Cause. Bending, forcing. Normal position.
   Head thrust forward. Cause. Forcing. Normal position.
   Wry neck. Surgical treatment.
Results of treatment on
   (1) Position of the head.
   (2) Muscles of the neck.
   (3) Fat or thin necks.
   (4) Nerves of the neck.
   (5) Circulation and dizziness.
   (6) Headache.
   (7) Secondary effects on thorax and shoulders.
Æsthetic. Nine realms, and meanings.
The alphabet: bending, turning, rolling, and forcing.
Important rules to members in treating defects :
   1st. *Remove the cause.*
   2d. *Bring the part to its normal position.*

THE LEGS.

Definition : Thigh, leg, knee, ankle, foot.
Thigh : Divisions : Front, back, out and inside.
Defects : Inner and back thigh not well developed.
Cause : Lack of training.
Results :

Treatment:
(1) *Front:* lower body; jump; run.
(2) *Biceps:* flex leg; raise heels in a run.
(3) *Inside:* cross legs.
(4) *Outside:* Take 1, 2, 3.

Legs: Parts, front and back. Better developed than thigh.
Defects: Small back.
Cause: Lack of exercise.
Results: General weakness.
Treatment:
(1) *Back:* Raise on toes. Running and jumping.
(2) *Front:* Raise the toes. Fast walking.

Knees: Definition. Defects. Treatment.
Ankle: Definition. Defects. Cause. Treatment.
The foot and toes.
The hips: Jumpers, wrestlers, horseback riders.

Compare the results of arm and leg work on circulation and respiration. Leg work produces better effects on brain congestion.

Alphabet: step, charge, hop, run, swing, sway, extend, flex, rotate.

THE ARMS.

Definition and division. Names of bones of arm (not wrist).
(1) *Deltoid.*
(2) *Upper arm*, front and back.
(3) *Forearm*, front and back.
Wrist, hand, fingers.

Defects: Forearm better developed than the upper in proportion.
Cause: Lack of exercise, over-development of certain parts.
Treatment:
(1) *Front upper:* flex forearm; rotate forearm.
(2) *Back upper:* thrust arm in any direction.

FIG. 5.—Turn Head, Wand Front Stepping. (Page 112.)

OUTLINE LESSONS ON PARTS OF THE BODY. 125

(3) *Front forearm:* flex hand and fingers; twist forearm.
(4) *Back forearm:* extend hand; extend fingers.
(5) *Wrist:* by all-hand motions; rotation and four bending motions.
(6) *Hand:* flex and extend fingers; Delsarte hand-shaking; separate fingers; fold fingers.

Use in cramp, paralysis, etc.
Effect of treatment on
- (1) Circulation.
- (2) Cold hands.
- (3) Respiration.
- (4) Headache.
- (5) Nerves.

Terms of alphabet: flex, rotate, thrust, twist, extend, separate, shaking.

THE ARM.

Free gymnastics do not, noticeably, increase the size of the muscles or bring great strengh. They add somewhat to the symmetry of the arm, however. Pupils notice this, and consequently do not care much for such movements as flexing, extending, swinging, or circling the arm, or opening and closing the hand. Nevertheless, it does not follow that because these exercises do not produce apparent results, we should eliminate them from our list. Strength is not the only result of physical training. This is illustrated in the development of the muscles of the arm. True, the hand, fingers, and forearm can be strengthened and developed, and in a very short time can be tired out, by free hand movements, but the biceps and the triceps are not exhausted so quickly. It is advisable, therefore, for the teacher to give special lessons for the development of the arms, using either the one-pound, wooden dumb bells a great number of times or the light iron dumb bells a few times.

It neither requires a thorough knowledge of anatomy to develop the muscles of the arms nor calls for much time to learn the specific exercises.

While we may urge our men to take certain preliminary exercises before developing the arm, we cannot compel them to do it. They will do about as they please, for physical education is not, like many other departments of education, compulsory. No harm will result if they begin the lesson with arm work. What is said about the development of the arm will apply with equal truth to the development of the muscles of the leg and thigh.

Let us study this wonderful part of the human body, the arm. The teacher knows the anatomical names of these bones, but at the start had better not say to a child that this bone is the radius, or that such and such a bone is the semi-lunar or the scaphoid bone. Attention is called to the divisions of the arm, as we shall treat them; first, the upper arm, which is subdivided into the front and the back. These are the parts of the upper arm to which we pay most attention in our general classes. Then comes the forearm, which is also subdivided into the front and the back. Passing from that part we come to the wrist, then the hand proper, and finally the fingers.

In developing the arm, pay more attention to the upper than to the forearm, for this reason: the forearm is usually better developed in proportion, because the hand

and the fingers are used so frequently. If you wish to strengthen some part of the arm, the question arises, What exercise shall we give for developing the muscles? The teacher who understands the principles for developing the parts of the body can apply them to the chest weights as well as to the special developing appliances. Let us take the upper arm. On the front part is the muscle called the biceps—the best-known muscle in the human body. Nearly every boy is familiar with it. He cares nothing for the origin and insertion of that muscle, but the teacher should. He knows, perhaps, that a certain exercise will develop the biceps; and if he does not know it he wishes that he did, and that he had a large muscle there. The two exercises for this part of the body are: first, flexing the forearm, second, with the arm partly flexed, rotating the forearm. Ask the boy to place his hand upon the biceps, then flex and rotate the forearm, that he may feel the muscle contract. It is an object lesson to him. He is also interested to know why a screw turns to the right and not to the left—why we can use more force in turning the hand in one direction than in the other; because the long, strong muscle on the upper arm helps to turn the right hand to the right.

Pass to the back of the upper arm, to what is called the triceps. If the child knows so well what the bicep muscle is, it is not harder for him to learn what the triceps is and where it is found. The chief exercise is the extension of the forearm. This muscle will push the hand away from the shoulder, or it will push the shoulder away from the hand. If, holding in the hand a dumb bell, we push it up, out, or front, the triceps is one of the muscles that do the work. Other muscles are always used; it is impossible to develop one particular muscle in the human body, but one muscle can get the greater part of the work and thus be strengthened.

Take next the deltoid, the "round-of-the-shoulder." Teachers of gymnastics should study this portion of the arm. The movement that develops this beautiful muscle is swinging the arm shoulder high, when its action stops. The arm is raised from the horizontal by the muscles which rotate the scapula, or the shoulder blade. In drawing the arm forward shoulder high, the anterior portion of the deltoid is called into action.

The forearm is subdivided into the front and back. The movement in free gymnastics for developing the front forearm is the flexing of the hand or the closing of the fingers. The exercise for the back forearm and for the back of the hand is the extension of the hand and fingers. A third exercise for the muscles of the forearm is twisting the hand from right to left. Although the biceps acts, it is assisted by muscles in the forearm, termed "pronators" and "supinators."

The wrist is strengthened and developed by the movements of the hand and the forearm. The extension and flexion, the abduction, adduction, and circumduction of the hand, are all good for the wrist.

Arm exercises are helpful in certain forms of headache, especially those due to temporary cerebral congestion resulting from study or too close mental application. These movements draw the blood from the brain to the upper extremities. It has been said by some teachers that they are able to remedy the pain in the head by the hand-shaking movements used in Delsarte gymnastics. We have found from experience that it is well to relieve cerebral pressure by arm or leg exercises. If it happens that the leg movements cannot be given in the schoolroom, use the arms. During continued mental effort the scholars should frequently be given exercises that will bring into action the muscles of the extremities.

There are, in all of our classes, pupils who suffer from cold hands and cold feet. One cause of this is the poor circulation through the parts. It is, of course, necessary. to strengthen the action of the heart and increase the lung capacity, to overcome this defect. At the same time, the circulation must be quickened through the parts themselves. The exercises for the hands and arms will tend to overcome this unfavorable condition.

People who have small arms, and who do not show the results of their gymnastic training in large measurements of this portion of the body, may find some consolation in the fact that the exercises develop the nerves. The musician has not, as a rule, a very large forearm. The muscles are well developed, elastic, and respond quickly to a stimulus sent to them. The nerves are in excellent condition, and it is here that we see the results of the training. It has been said before that muscles need not be large to be strong. If there is, back of a fair muscular condition, a great deal of nervous energy and will power, the muscles will do the work.

The teachers of elocution in our colleges and secondary schools complain of the awkwardness of their pupils in making gestures, or in expressing emotions by the body.

The small boy, speaking his piece from a platform in the school, considers that he has accomplished quite a feat if he swings his arm forward or to the right or left, in his effort to make a gesture. The instructor in gymnastics will be able to assist the teacher of elocution if she will drill the scholars in certain arm and shoulder movements when in the gymnasium. The swinging of the arm to the front, from this position out, then down, or swinging the arm up, out, and down, will very soon produce greater freedom of movement at the shoulder joint. The angles can soon be turned into curves, so that, by constant practice, the child will be enabled, by use of the arms, shoulders, head, and body, to make gestures and to express his emotions when speaking.

The child who begins the five-finger exercises on the piano will soon be able to play octaves, the chords, and the most difficult pieces; but we do not find, as the child grows older and continues his practice, that there is a great increase in the size of the muscle. The quality, if not the quantity, is there.

THE SHOULDERS.

Definition and anatomy. Technical and common names.
Capable of all motions.
Defects:
    (1) Round.
    (2) Uneven.
    (3) Stooped.
    (4) Sloping.
Results of these defects on the thorax and health.
Theory of treatment. See rules under "The Head."
Treatment by primary and secondary exercises.
Round shoulders. Cause. Treatment.

Primary :
- (1) Force.
- (2) Elevate or raise.
- (3) Depress or lower.
- (4) Roll.

Secondary :
- (1) Setting up exercises.
- (2) Circling motion backward with arms.
- (3) Attitudes, good. Hips firm. Neck firm. Letter "Y." Attention.
- (4) Attitudes, bad. Arms folded. Incorrect sitting, standing, or lying positions.

Stooped shoulders is a defect in the spine, and will be treated under the heading "Spine."

Uneven shoulders. Cause. Treatment.
    To elevate, shrug or elevate the lower shoulder as a primary motion.

Secondary :
    Arm swinging out or up ; arm thrusting up ; head bending to high side.

To lower a shoulder, *thrust arm down; force shoulder down.*

Bottle neck, or sloping. Cause.

General rules for treatment :
- (1) Widen and deepen chest.
- (2) Build up neck muscles.
- (3) Elevate shoulders.

Secondary effects of the shoulder work is to widen and deepen the thorax.

Results on respiration.

Æsthetic work.
    Value of shoulder work in elocution.
    Shoulder, the thermometer of the feelings.
    Combination of shoulder and head motions.

Terms of the alphabet used : raise, lower, force, roll, circling, swinging, thrusting.

It is difficult to determine whether drooping heads or

round shoulders are the more common. We know there are too many of each. As a rule, the attention of parents is attracted to round shoulders sooner than to a drooping head. The teacher of gymnastics will have more requests from parents for exercises to remedy round shoulders than for those which affect the position of the head. Of the two, the defective shoulder is the more serious, because it affects directly the diameters of the thorax.

The anatomy of the shoulder joint is simple. It is composed of three bones, the scapula, clavicle, and humerus; or, in ordinary language, the shoulder blade, the collar bone, and upper arm. (It may be well to state here that it is not wise for a teacher to use technical terms too frequently before a class. It may awe the children for a short time, but with adults it generally produces a feeling of disgust; it seems to older pupils as if the teacher were trying to "air" her knowledge—to show her superior wisdom by using phrases unintelligible to them.)

The shoulder joint is capable of nearly every motion. It can be raised or lowered, thrust forward or back, rolled, adducted, or abducted. The peculiarity of the shoulder blade is that it is practically suspended. This being the case, it is plain that if one set of muscles is over-developed, it will draw the shoulder in their pulling direction. To illustrate: if the large pectoral muscles, which connect the shoulder with the breast-bone, are stronger than the muscles on the back, the shoulder will be drawn forward, producing the common defect of round shoulders. For similar reasons, one shoulder may be higher than the other, or the spine itself may be drawn slightly forward in the region of the shoulders, producing what is called "stooped shoulders."

Let us consider the first of these defects, round shoulders. This is due to over-development of the muscles of the front upper thorax, to posture, or to occupation. The scholar who sits with arms resting on the desk, or lies in bed in such a position as to draw the shoulders forward, is producing this defect. The result is that the chest is flattened and the appearance of the shoulders changed. Any movements or postures that shorten the diameters of the thorax should be avoided, because the free action of the heart and lungs must never be impeded.

In treating this defect, the general rule is to bring the shoulders to their proper position. This in itself is the most important of the primary exercises. All secondary exercises are taken with the arms, head, and trunk. In the case of round shoulders, the first primary exercise would be to draw the shoulders back, the second would be to arch the chest, the third to touch the inner borders of the scapula, the fourth to roll the shoulders back, emphasizing the backward but not the forward motion. Under the secondary exercises we would enumerate the "setting up exercises," or any movement with the arms that will tend to bring the scapula to the normal position.

Uneven shoulders are caused by the over-development of muscles on one side of the body, by posture, or by occupation. Right-handed people are stronger on the right side of the body than on the left. In nearly every case examined the left shoulder is higher than the right. Pupils who carry books on the right arm, or who stand with one hip higher than the other, are apt to show this defect.

The general plan of treatment is simple; if the shoulder is too low, raise it, if too high, lower it. These are primary exercises. Thrusting the flexed arm up and swinging the arm up are secondary exercises. A good combination would be to flex both arms, and from this position thrust one hand up and the other down.

In the case of a bottle-necked pupil, the shoulder treatment is of less importance than the treatment of the thorax.

Stooped shoulders will be considered under the heading of the spine, as this defect is due to a curve in the vertebral column. It is much more difficult to cure for this reason.

The effect of these exercises upon the thorax, as has been stated, is to widen and deepen it. The circulation and respiration are therefore benefited. Widening and deepening the thorax will of course increase the size of the abdominal cavity, thus shoulder exercises aid, indirectly, digestion.

The above brief description of the shoulders will give the teacher some idea of the plan used by the author in filling out a skeleton lecture.

THE THORAX AND ITS CONTENTS.

Thorax—Definition. Anatomy. Contents.
What constitutes a normal thorax?
Defective thorax: Uneven, short diameters.
Cause: Dress, position, pressure, lack of exercise.

Results of defects on
  Lungs, heart, waist.
Treatment:
  (1) By external and internal development.
  (2) Of heart.
  (3) Of lungs.
The external treatment is to widen and deepen.
  To widen: Primary:
      "Sternum expression."
      Force back abdomen.
    Secondary:
      Shrug shoulders.
      Swing arm sidewise.
      Bend body to right and left.
      Bend body to right and left, neck firm.
      Bend body, arms (1 or 2) up.
      Letter "Y."
  To deepen: Primary:
      "Sternum expression."
    Secondary:
      Bend back head.
      Bend body back and to oblique.
      Swing arms front and up.
      Letter "Y" and back bend.
      Hips firm and forward bend.
Terms of alphabet: force, shrug, swing, bend.

THORAX—BREATHING.

The lungs.
Definition.
Importance of exercise.
Exercise for lungs:
  Why do we breathe?
  How do we breathe?
Defects:
  Lungs partly filled.

Kinds:
  Diaphragmatic.
  Intercostal.
  Abdominal.
  Chest.
What muscles are used in breathing?
Two parts of breathing: inhaling and exhaling.
Normal breathing. See a child.
Abnormal breathing. When it begins. Corset. Dress.
Breathing of civilized men and women and of Indian women. See Kirke's "Physiology."
Treatment: inhaling is primary.
Secondary:
  (1) Combine with head bending.
  (2) Arm motions to side and front.
  (3) Inhale and arm forcing. Percussing.
  (4) Shrug and force shoulders.
  (5) Trunk bending.
  (6) Exercises for one side.
Which deepen or widen?
Leg vs. arm work.
Describe the action of the lungs when one is asleep, sitting, standing, running.

Breathing in Ling laws. Why begin slowly. Simple breathing for children. Whistle, sing, hiss. Breathlessness vs. fatigue. Effects of breathing on circulation. Reflex action in speaking, fear, anger. School ventilation.

Terms of alphabet: breathing, percussing, shrugging, bending, forcing.

Any good work on anatomy will assist the teacher in studying the formation of the thorax, while the various works on physiology will tell of the action of the muscles and the functions of the organs in this portion of the body. It is not our intention to describe the anatomy and physiology of the parts, but to give the teacher a few suggestions for the development of this very important portion of the body.

By the thorax, we refer to that bony, cartilaginous cage which is bounded in front by the sternum and the ribs, on the sides by the ribs, at the back by the spinal column and the ribs, and at its base by the diaphragm. The portions of the body found in the thorax are the heart and lungs, with their appendages. These organs are directly affected by physical training, and suffer from a lack of care.

It is not easy to answer the question, "What constitutes a normal thorax?" There are certain measurements that will be of service, if we depended upon figures. There is not so much data for children. We should expect to find a healthy thorax in a healthy child. The diameters from front to rear, and from right to left, are not shortened too much. It may be that the upper portion of this cage is too small, in which case we should endeavor to widen and deepen that part. We are not liable to make a mistake in widening and deepening the thorax to too great an extent.

There are certain gymnastic movements that will develop the chest, but before any defect can be remedied we must, if possible, ascertain its cause and remove it. Any other course would be as absurd as for a person to hold in the hand a hot coal and try to remedy the effects without removing the heat. If the defective thorax is caused by improper dress, change it. If it is the result of a bad standing position, correct the position. If it is due to pressure—by this we mean the leaning against a desk, or the occupation of the person, carrying weights, etc.—

remove the pressure. If the diameters are shortened because of weakened muscles, and the muscles are weakened through lack of exercise, give the child gymnastics. The results of the defects in the thorax are shown in the action of the lungs, heart, and the abdominal organs. If the heart has not ample space, it cannot perform its functions. If the lungs are crowded, they cannot aërate the blood. If the lower diameters of the thorax are small the waist will be the same, hence there is not room for the action of the organs of the abdomen that is required of them to perform their special functions.

The development of the thorax may be secured in three ways : first, by external and internal muscular development; second, by exercises which increase the size of the heart; and, third, by the development of the lungs. Under the first heading, we may subdivide the external treatment into two kinds of movements—primary and secondary, the object of these movements being to widen and deepen the chest. The chest and thorax in this case are synonymous, although (in the eyes of physical directors) the chest muscles and the muscles of the thorax are not identical. The primary motion for widening the chest is that in which the thorax itself is used to produce the result. Mr. Roberts, the energetic instructor in gymnastics in the Boston Y. M. C. A., has termed this movement " sternum expression." It consists in the arching of the chest—the elevation of the ribs. It is performed by forcing back the anterior walls of the abdomen and depressing somewhat the shoulders. The question may then be properly asked, Is this a primary exercise for the thorax, if other parts are used to produce the result? It is the nearest approach to a primary motion we can call to mind. It certainly has great value. If the mouth and nose are closed the pupil can, by pure muscular movement, increase the girth measurements one or two inches.

The secondary exercises for widening the thorax are these : shrug or elevate the shoulders as high as possible ; swing the arms sideways over the head, with neck firm or arms up, bend the body to the right and left, or, by placing one hand on the hip and curving the other hand over the head, bending the body to one side, we elevate the opposite portion of the thorax. The letter Y position (Fig. 6) will also widen the chest.

To deepen the thorax there is but one primary motion, which has been described under the term "sternum expression." The secondary movements are : the bending backward of the head, the bending of the body backward and obliquely backward, the swinging of the arms forward and upward, the letter Y position and body bending backward, the hips firm, chest arched, and body bending forward. It is not the object of this chapter to go into a complete list of movements or to arrange a progressive series of exercises. It is well, however, for the teacher to understand the principles upon which the movements are based. Baron Posse's "Swedish Gymnastics" (Kinesiology) is strongly indorsed.

The instructor who wishes, can ascertain the results of arm movements on the diameters of the thorax by placing the calipers against the walls of the chest, then swinging the arms sideways and upward. By so doing she will find that the diameter is increased very perceptibly. This is equally true if the calipers are placed against the spine and the anterior portion of the thorax, and the arms raised forward.

There has been some discussion lately on the comparative value of certain exercises for widening and deepening the thorax. It seems that many of our gymnastic teachers have accepted without question the statement that the quarter circle, intercostal machine, and abdominal attachment to the chest weight are the instruments, *par excellence*, for widening and deepening the chest.

The student anxious to deepen his chest has been advised to lie over the arc of the quarter circle and go through prescribed movements, or if this was not available to use the intercostal machine. In case the second device was also wanting, the instructor recommended the plan shown in the following illustration; a simple combination of the abdominal attachment of the chest weight and a mat.

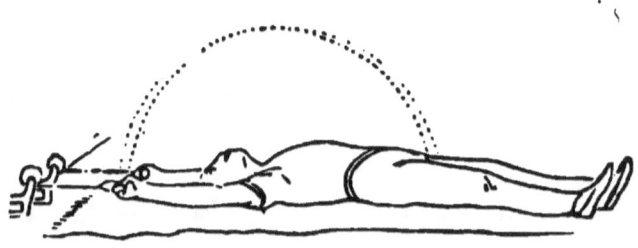

Almost ten years ago a firm interested in the manufacture of gymnastic apparatus distributed an illustrated pamphlet on the chest weight; since then nearly every firm engaged in making appliances for the gymnasium has used identical cuts, with the same descriptive wording, while usage and habit have made the diagrams seem correct.

It will be beneficial to the cause of physical training if more time can be given to thoughtful discussion of the apparatus found in our modern gymnasia. Some teachers take too much for granted, they are slow in taking the initiative in investigating statements; others blindly pin their faith to manuals issued by publishers.

The raising of the arms sideways and upwards widens the chest, while swinging them forward and upward deepens it. This statement is easily verified by the application of the slide or calipers.

Arm-raising is done by muscles above the shoulders and on the upper back, so that the result of these movements, *i. e.*, the lengthening of the diameters of the thorax, is accomplished by the muscles that *elevate* the shoulders, ribs, and arms.

To produce a like effect we have been in the habit of placing the student on the quarter circle, requiring him to develop the muscles which pull *down* or depress the shoulders, ribs, and arms.

Now the question arises, Why do we at one moment give arm-raising with or without resistance to expand the chest and the next direct the pupil to pull the arms down to reach the same result? It has been said that the pectorals in this exercise will elevate the sternum; this would be so if the shoulders were firmly fixed, but of the two parts of the body, the shoulders move more readily and are consequently drawn forward and down. A broad, deep chest does not usually accompany round, sloping shoulders.

In the treatment of "the bony cartilaginous cage," we place too little value upon the development of the middle back, and the position of the spine. It is of great importance that the vertebræ be kept as nearly as possible within the line of their customary curves.

Correct posture is soon to play a more important part in our gymnastic training.

Why is it that if we wish to produce a normal back we place the pupil in a very abnormal position and *keep him there*, as on the quarter circle? It is hardly rational to expect to produce symmetry by assuming and holding positions that approach deformity. (Exceptions are made when treating scoliosis, etc.)

The quarter circle is a clever device for strengthening the front and sides of the waist and the abdomen; it is valuable for certain forms of indigestion, and may be of use in reducing adipose, but as a chest deepener it is over-rated. It is true that by placing a person over the curved board, the chest is arched, and if the patient will grasp the handles and allow the hands to go slowly back and up, there is a perceptible increase in the girth measurement; but is this increase the result of the contraction of the muscles themselves, or is it the effect of the weight? If the latter, then the chest is expanded by a weight and not by muscular contraction, and if this is true, would not the muscles which prevent expansion of the chest be strengthened in their effort to overcome the resistance made by the weight?

To permanently expand the thorax we must develop the *muscles* which produce this result.

The quarter circle develops the recti, external and

FIG. 7.—The Chest Machine. (Page 143.)

internal oblique abdominal and transversalis muscles.

Muscles tend to draw their points of origin and insertion toward each other even when at rest. How, then, can these strong bands which are drawing the anterior portion of the thorax and the pelvic attachment nearer together assist in deepening the chest?

The strong latissimi also draw down. By which method, then, are we to elevate the chest? By continually working downward or upward?

The same may be asked in reference to the intercostal and abdominal attachment of the chest weight.

The belief that a machine built upon the reverse order would be productive of better results led me to fashion an inclined board with wheels at the base, so planned that the chest would be properly arched and kept so during the exercise. This can be done by a device that will support the middle upper back and prevent any sinking or sagging of the spine.

The illustration (Fig. 7) gives one an idea of the new chest machine. The roller is adjustable, adapting the machine to persons of different heights. Some changes will be made in the details. The wheels near the weights are not needed, and instead of a roller, will be used an oblong back rest or curved board.

The following deductions have also led me to depart from the beaten path :

1. The position on the old quarter circle is not a good one.

2. The machine is essentially for the waist and abdomen and not the chest, while the muscles that should be developed are not drawn enough into action.

3. The force is from above down, consequently the muscles developed tend to cramp the thorax by pulling it lower.

By the new device:

1. The pupil is placed in a posture that approximates a normal position of the body, the surface of the board being molded to the spinal curves and tilted back far enough to localize the work. On this board one cannot exaggerate the attitude, but is compelled to arch the chest to nearer the right degree.

2. The muscles which tend to compress the thorax are not brought into action as on the old machine, while those instrumental in widening the chest are developed.

3. In the old quarter circle the *weights* deepen the chest; here the *muscles* do the work, and are made stronger by overcoming resistance from below.

In applying the principle to the intercostal machine, I have followed the same plan, in that the wheels are placed on the floor, consequently the pulling is from below upward, while with the abdominal mat the pupil lies at length with his feet, not his head, to the machine.

I do not say that the new chest machine is the best contrivance in the gymnasium for expanding the thorax, for I am of the opinion that the inverted "Intercostal" is preferable, but I think that of the two machines for developing the chest, the quarter circle and new chest machine, the latter is better.

The research work done by the pupils of the Anderson School of Gymnastics in reference to this subject led me to believe that the principle of continually *pulling down* to increase the thoracic diameter is wrong.

BREATHING.

A subject that should be discussed under the heading Thorax. The importance attached to the development of the lungs cannot be questioned. The teacher should know what exercises are used, how they affect the lungs; she should understand why we breathe, and how we breathe. If the opportunity presents itself, it would be to the advantage of the teacher to make some device that will show the scholars the method of breathing. Dr. Seaver, of the Yale Gymnasium, has arranged a device with bellows, that answers this purpose admirably. Pupils do not understand that the lungs are filled by having a vacuum produced, into which the air rushes.

The defects in the lungs are these: the upper portions of the apices are not, as a rule, filled at each inhalation. People who live a sedentary life do not call into action the necessary portions of the lung, which, if not used, may become weakened and diseased. Scholars who will not take the breathing exercises of their own accord should be made to breathe deeply and rapidly through the exercises set aside for this purpose, viz.: running, jumping, or quick leg work of any kind.

It is not wise for the teacher to discuss the different forms of breathing with small children. It is of little moment to a child whether its breathing is diaphragmatic, intercostal, abdominal, or thoracic—or what muscles are used. The teacher should, at every lesson, give some drill that will compel the child to breathe deeply and rapidly.

In reply to the question, What muscles are used in breathing, we can say that nearly every muscle of the body is used in forced inspiration. In the ordinary breathing, the muscles surrounding the thorax play an important part. But here, as before, the teacher can learn by referring to the works on anatomy and physiology. The difference in length of inhaling and exhaling is discussed in the works on the physiology of exercise. The chapter on breathlessness in La Grange's "Physiology of Exercise" is very interesting. The teacher who wishes to ascertain the difference between normal and abnormal breathing should study the healthy child. Abnormal breathing begins when the action of the thorax is interfered with by dress, posture, profession, or disease. The breathing of men and women should be identical. The experiments made by Dr. Mays of Philadelphia, Dr. Robert L. Dickinson of Brooklyn, and Dr. Kellogg of Battle Creek will give the reader further information on this subject. Instructors in gymnastics, whether physicians or laymen, should read articles on the lungs, their diseases and treatment.

To increase the capacity of the lungs, the primary work would be inhaling and exhaling. The secondary would be a combination of inhaling with the head bending movements backward, the arm swinging sideways and upward, or artificial respiration, which is performed after this fashion : the arms are raised forward and upward, during which time the pupil inhales; they are then forced backward and downward, when exhalation takes place. The teacher should notice the position of the head and the hips during these movements. Shrugging or elevating the shoulders combined with breathing is a good exercise. Inhaling, holding the breath for a few seconds, and gently forcing the arms (which are half flexed) backward, is also a good drill.

The general rules for increasing the capacity of the lungs would be these: give all running, jumping, hopping, and leaping movements; give the class drills in counting aloud, singing, and whistling. Make the work simple, but interesting, when teaching children. They love to take these movements.

THE SPINE.

There has been a constant call for exercises that will remedy or cure certain defects of the spine. We cannot lay down a series of rules and say that they will apply to all cases. Physicians who have had experience in handling the spine are careful about preparing set rules or exercises for abnormal curves. The common defect in the spine termed kyphosis, or, in plain words, stooping shoulders, will be helped by the following exercises.

KYPHOSIS.—A SERIES OF EXERCISES FOR KYPHOSIS, OR STOOPING SHOULDERS.

Assume the best possible standing position, with head erect, chest arched, hips back.

(1) *Neck work.* Clasp the hands back of the head, then pulling with the hands, bend head backward, eight to sixteen times.

(2) *Shoulder work.* Swing the arms forward and upward, then force them back and down six to eight times.

(3) *Back work.* With the arms up bend the body well forward, keeping the arms at the side of the head, eight times.

(4) Same as No. 3, but in the kneeling position. Also bend the body backward.

(5) *Neck work.* Lie, face downward, on the floor or mat, resting forehead on the folded arms. Raise head as high as possible eight to sixteen times.

(6) *Upper spine.* With the neck firm, position lying face down, some one holding the feet, raise the shoulders as high as possible one to ten times.

(7) "*Swimming motion.*"

In case the exercises are too severe take each one only a few times and omit Nos. 6 and 7.

These exercises are to be taken the number of times indicated by the figures.

The swimming motion is taken in this way : lie face down, as in No. 5, but go through regular swimming motions with the arms. The hands are not to touch the floor at any time. These exercises are also good for drooping head.

Projecting hips may be helped if the teacher will give to the scholars exercises for developing the muscles on the front and sides of the waist, the anterior portion of the pelvis, and the upper front thighs. If any special rule were to be given for the treatment of a spinal defect, it would be to place the patient in the best possible position, compelling him to hold it until slightly fatigued, then permitting rest, and later on repeating the process. If defects are caused by incorrect posture, they can be helped by assuming and holding correct positions. If a bad position produces a defect, a good position will tend to cure it. It would be far better for the instructor in gymnastics who has not a medical education to refer a case of spinal trouble or defect to some physician.

COMMON PHYSICAL DEFECTS.

The common physical defects which may be helped by free gymnastics :

Head.
> Drops forward.
> Carried a little to one side.
> Chin raised too high, or protruding.

Shoulders.
> Round, stooping, sloping, and uneven.

Thorax.
> One side better developed or larger than the other.
> The diameters too short.

Upper back.
> Right shoulder blade too prominent in right-handed people.

Spine.
> Side or lateral curves. Rotation.
> Bends too far forward from between the shoulders.

Waist.
> Too narrow.
> Abdominal muscles weak.

Hips.
> Thrown too far forward.

Arms.
> Forearm better developed than the upper arm.

Leg.
> Better developed than thigh.

Thigh.
> Inside and back poorly developed.

Planes of the Body. The arms may be held shoulder high to the side, front, or obliquely front ; hip high to side; head high to side. To distinguish the position of straight arms, these planes of the body are used: head, shoulders, chest, and hips.

Directions. All exercises are given in one or more of the following directions: down, out, up, or front. Or they may be given to the front and back, right and left, and in the oblique directions front and back, both to right and left.

CHAPTER XII.

HOW TO TEACH WALKING.

BEFORE walking can be taught, there must be a thorough comprehension of what is meant by good walking. No man or woman can teach what he or she does not know, and if what constitutes good walking is not understood, the instructor cannot teach.

A preliminary talk with children invariably has an excellent effect, when the subject of walking is to be brought to their attention. Ask them to notice how a minister walks up the church aisle and into his pulpit. They will readily see your point when you state that the deliberate, measured step he takes detracts not at all, but is associated with the dignity of his office. They will agree with you when you say that the joyousness of a laughing child finds outward expression in a light, quick walk; that imbecility is evinced by an undecided walk, wavering and weak. Old age totters and requires support. An honest, courageous, active young man or woman may walk well, and a person would be far more likely to trust one with such a walk than the individual who entered his presence with a shuffling, shambling gait. Many a child has not, before this, really comprehended that carriage and the walk are closely allied with the character. Pride in self is aroused, the incentive to be a noble-looking and noble-acting boy or girl comes forth, and before the "practical teaching" is begun the child wants to walk correctly, and *will*, if you teach it rightly.

Ask your pupils to watch an ideal walker. Tell them that such a person is a good walker, being easy and graceful, the opposite of awkward and clumsy, in his movements. Tell them to observe that Mr. B. carries his body properly, this including the position of the head, the chest, and the hips. If the child observes that the head droops forward, that the chest is flat, or the hips are too far advanced, he knows that these defects must be remedied before good walking can be acquired. The public school-teacher, anxious to train her pupils in this art, should watch them carefully, taking into consideration the position of the head, the action of the shoulders, hips, legs, and arms. The carriage of the body as a whole should be observed.

In teaching the exercises it will not only be necessary to note carefully the defects which exist, but the various movements of the different parts of the body must be carefully analyzed, as a person takes a few steps. Again, the members of the body must be trained as parts, and then we must apply the exercises to the body as a whole. A child may use his arms well, if he uses only the arms. He may have free leg movements, his head may be erect, the chest may be beautifully arched; but it requires practice to properly handle all of these different parts at once, as in walking. It is not possible to make a perfect whole from imperfect parts. Nor is it possible to make a perfect whole of perfect parts, unless they are rightly placed together. Therefore, not only should the members of the body which are used be educated, but the body as a whole should be brought under discipline.

The right carriage of the head and chest adds dignity to the walk. Call to the pupil's attention the necessity of holding the head erect. It will become evident to the observing teacher that some pupils swing the head too much in walking. Others thrust the head forward, or give to the shoulders a swinging or shrugging movement. The arms of some scholars are held stiffly at the side, or are not allowed to swing at all. There may be a sinking motion to the hip, as the pupil takes a step. The foot may be placed heavily upon the floor. The start may be made from the flat foot and not from the ball of the foot, or the walking itself may be unsteady and in irregular lines. Now, knowing these defects, the next thing is to analyze two or three steps, that we may secure exercises to assist in teaching pupils how to walk.

The pupil starts from the position of attention (Fig. 8), the weight equally distributed upon both feet. From this attitude it is impossible to take a step without doing two things: first, the body must sway to the right, that the left foot may be free; and, second, the body must fall forward, that the pupil may gain ground or advance. Since this is true, we know that at first there are two movements which can be given as exercises:

SWAYING EXERCISES.

1. With common base, sway the body from the right to the left. Allow four counts to the right and four to the left. (The effect of this exercise, when taken by a

large class, is rather pleasing, as it brings a suggestion of the wheat in the field, as it is swayed gently to and fro by the wind.)

Sway the body forward and backward, using the common base. (This will be a more difficult exercise, as the arc of the circle made by the head is shorter than from right to left. In either of these exercises do not bend the body, but let it sway as a whole.) To modify the movements, place the right foot its length obliquely forward to the right and sway to the forward foot, raising slightly the back heel. Sway back to the left foot, leaving the right foot on the floor. The motion should be even and regular. Also sway the body to the right and left with a wide base, the feet eight to ten inches apart. (The pupil who makes quick and jerky motions in these exercises will be apt to do the same in walking.)

After swaying, the next noticeable movement is bending the left knee, preparatory to raising the left foot from the floor.

KNEE BENDING EXERCISES.

2. Without removing the toes from the floor, slightly bend the right knee from eight to sixteen times, and then the left. Notice whether the pupil allows the right hip to sink when taking the knee bendings. This, if it occurs, is a defect. The child who lowers the hip while practicing the knee bending exercises may do the same in walking. (See Fig. 9.)

FOOT RAISING EXERCISES.

3. Without moving other parts of the body, half flex the right thigh sixteen times. Take the same exercise

with the left. By this means the foot is raised from the floor.

After the foot has been raised from the floor by flexing the thigh, it is necessary, to gain ground, to swing the leg forward. As a means to this end give the leg swinging exercises. (Note the difference between the leg and the thigh.) The teacher will observe that this is a balancing motion.

LEG SWINGING EXERCISES.

4. With the thigh slightly flexed, swing the leg forward and backward eight or sixteen times, keeping the thigh in place.

After the leg swings forward, and the foot is made ready to be placed on the floor, give the extending and flexing of the foot.

FOOT EXTENSION AND FLEXION EXERCISE.

5. Extend and flex the right foot eight or sixteen times. The left.

The teacher will notice now, that the weight of the body is upon the right leg, the foot of the left is ready to be placed upon the floor, and the next exercise which will naturally follow is changing the weight of the body from the right to the left foot.

CHANGING WEIGHT EXERCISE.

6. Let the body fall forward until its weight rests upon the left foot. Raise the heel of the right foot, the right toe touching the floor. Sway back again to the right foot, raising the left foot from the floor. Repeat this movement, going forward and back eight or sixteen times. (The feet do not come together in the exercise.)

The weight is now upon the left leg. The next exercise will be a pendulum movement. Give as an exercise thigh swinging forward and backward.

THIGH SWINGING EXERCISE.

7. Swing the thigh forward or backward eight or sixteen times with a pendulum motion.

A final exercise will require the movement of the body as a whole.

EXERCISE.

8. With the left foot take one step forward, planting the right foot by it, touching heels. Step back with right foot, bring the left back alongside it. Repeat to counts of eight or sixteen.

These exercises are termed primary, because they are actual parts of the step. To walk properly, the pupil should be able to balance the body well. As a secondary exercise, give balancing movements. Drill the pupil also in the charging, stepping, and wide base swaying movements. Running in place, and hopping and jumping movements are all valuable. If these are correctly done, the pupil will be taught to depend more upon the action of the ball of the foot than he does.

The foregoing is a description of exercises for the legs. A person must pay attention to the position of other parts of the body. Exercises should be given for widening and deepening the chest, for developing the muscles of the neck, that the head may be carried properly, for removing the tension from the arm muscles if it is too great, and for the strengthening of the waist and abdomen.

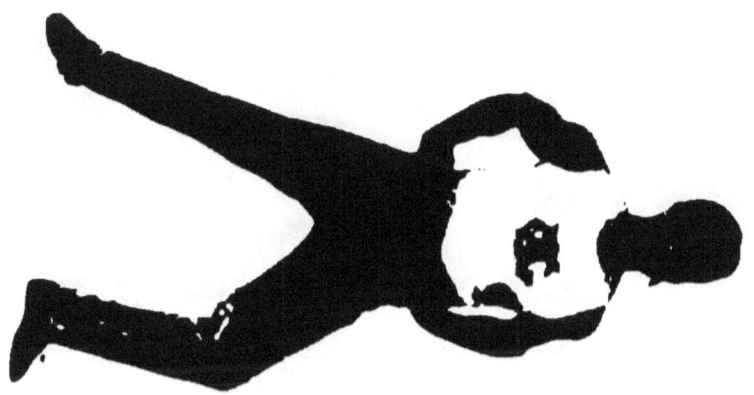

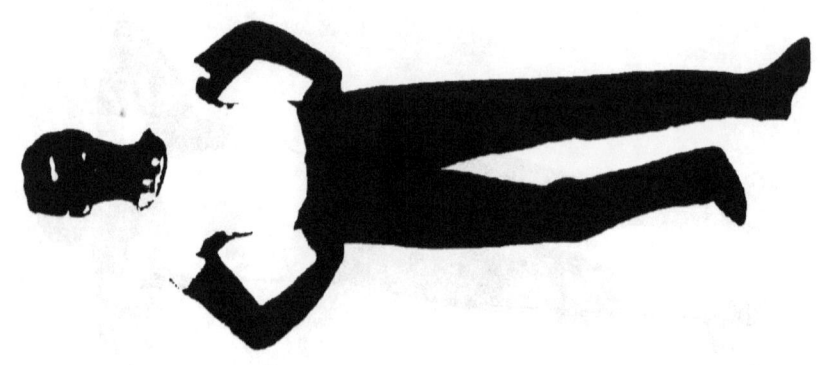

A few general rules will be of some value, if they are enforced. The ball of the foot does not touch the floor first. The best walkers plant almost a flat foot, the heel striking the ground a little in advance of the rest of the foot. Bean bags and light weights may be carried on the head. Do not overtrain one part of the body.

All exercises can be taken to waltz time; if music is not used the motions can be taken any odd or even number of times.

CHAPTER XIII.

THE ALPHABET.

SPACE will be given to a discussion of some of the letters of the alphabet. We use only twenty in our work, although there are other movements that can be classed under this head, but we find from experience that this number is sufficient for the present. Here we shall call attention to only a few of them.

Let us take up the first one, the stepping motion.* The *stepping motion*, which is a leg exercise, consists in swinging the leg forward until the foot has gone its own length, then touching the tip of the foot to the floor without lowering the heel. The foot is then returned and placed alongside the other. (See Fig. 10.) In this exercise the body is kept in place by balancing it on the left foot. The teacher should notice that the shoulders and thorax do not move. In short, the scholar should be kept in the position of attention, except that the right foot and leg are advanced, the weight being on the left.

The stepping motion is taken in these directions: to the front, obliquely forward, to the right, obliquely back, and back, the knee not being bent; but when taken across in front, to the left, or across back, the knee is bent. The tip of the toe touches the floor, and the angle

---
*The reader is referred to the work entitled "Light Gymnastics," by the author, for a short description of each of these terms.

kept by the feet is, in nearly all cases, sixty degrees. This is an important point to be remembered, otherwise the child is apt to "toe in," when stepping across.

Do not give more than the stepping exercise at one lesson, and thoroughly drill the scholars upon the movement. It will be found later, when teaching series of movements, that the stepping exercise forms an important part of many drills. Stepping and foot placing are not identical.

The charging motion is considered one of the most difficult movements in the alphabet. In the stepping motion the foot is carried forward its own length; in the charging motion twice its own length. Some instructors place the foot three lengths forward; we find two lengths sufficient. The body is carried forward, the trunk being in a perpendicular position, the heels and toes of both feet are on the floor, the right knee is bent until it conceals the foot. The point of the body farthest forward is the right knee, next the toes of the right foot, next the chest. The hands may be placed on the hip, the shoulders are turned a little to the right. The eyes are to the front, or they may be turned in the oblique direction and the head turned in the same way, if the teacher wishes. (See Fig. 11.)

The difficult parts of the charging motion are these: the chest must be in advance of the hips, the right knee is bent, the left leg is perfectly straight, and the lines which run from the right knee to the heel and from the left hip to the heel would be parallel in this motion. This last rule cannot be applied when the right foot is charged obliquely forward or backward to the left.

A charging motion is taken in seven directions, viz.: to the front and to the rear, obliquely forward and backward to the right and left, and to the right. We do not give the charging motion with the right foot to the left.

When teaching the stepping or charging motion notice that the first movement made by the body is a slight swaying motion to the left if the right foot is advanced.

In teaching the charging motion request the pupils to take a foot placing two foot lengths in a given direction, as seen in the illustration (Fig. 12), then bend the front knee, until the rule will apply.

In exercises of this character, when the eyes and shoulders are to the front, the feet preserve the angle of sixty degrees, when charging to the right or left and turning the shoulders in the same direction the foot points to the right or left. In this case the angle is greater than sixty degrees.

How to give the commands: For a stepping exercise say, "Stepping motion (or charging motion), right foot to the right, eight times, waltz time, *begin*." Generally state first what the exercise is to be and always leave the command of execution to the last.

The reverse charge. An exercise which is in many respects the reverse of the charging motion. It will be seen in the illustration. (See Fig. 13.)

The body is not carried forward but is slightly lowered, the right leg or foot is advanced twice its length, the left knee is bent, both feet are on the floor.

The defects to be remedied are these: the weight is carried too far forward, the feet do not rest on the floor according to the rule, the body may be turned too much

THE ALPHABET. 161

to one side. The motion is made in these directions: front, obliquely front, to the right, obliquely back, and back. The reverse charge is easier than the regular charging motion. The command is, "Reverse charge, the right foot to the front, *begin.*" State the direction and number of times.

Placing. A term applied to the feet and arms or the body as a whole. The foot is placed to the right or the front according to the rules found in the various manuals of Swedish gymnastics. The distance is either one or two foot lengths, the weight is equally divided after placing the foot. (See Fig. 14.) The command is, "Foot placing, right foot to the right (or left), one length (or two), *place.*" The term is applied to the arms or hands when they are to be placed on the hips, chest, or shoulders, or upon the shoulders of another.

Swaying motions. These are made with a common or wide base, by changing the weight from one foot to the other with or without knee bending. The command is, "Swaying motion, right foot charge (or place) to the right, *begin.*"

Swinging motions are made with the arms and legs, and consist in swinging them to some given height in a given direction. The command is, "Swing the arm out (or front or up), *begin.*"

Circling motions are different from the swinging motions. The term is applied to movements made with Indian clubs or to the similar exercises made with bells. Circles are made, not pendulum movements. The command is, "Circle the right club to the left (or right), *begin*"; or, "Shoulder circle to the right, *begin.*"

Thrusting and extending are the same.

Flexing and bending are the same.

These letters of the alphabet are described in "Light Gymnastics."

The lunging motions. The first is the three-quarter lunge, in which case the foot is carried forward three times its own length; second, the regulation lunge, as used in fencing. In many drills men prefer the three-quarter lunge and make the charging motion the same distance. It is necessary, nevertheless, that the class should be well trained in the full fencing lunge (four foot lengths). The first of these movements is given in as many directions as the charging motion. The second is given in but one direction—to the front. Do not give the full lunge to beginners. The command is similar to that for charging.

Hopping. It is not necessary to pay much attention to this exercise, as it is easily learned. It consists of leaping up and down, landing on the ball of the foot. The heel is not brought in contact with the floor. The teacher should instruct the scholars to hop as lightly as possible and not to jar the body.

The hopping movements are given either upon the right, upon the left, or upon both feet, while a pleasant variation is found in allowing the scholars to hop in the air, separate the feet, and land with a wide base, to hop again in the air, touch the heels, and come down in the starting position. The wide base may be made with the feet placed sidewise, or one foot forward and the other backward. The command is, "Hopping, on the right (or left) foot (so many times), *hop.*"

Running. There is little trouble in teaching running to boys and girls when young. In the gymnasium small girls will run as gracefully and as well as boys, but they have not the strength or the staying power. After a certain age, however, the girl seems to forget the use of her arms, and runs with an awkward gait that must result from the arms being held rigidly at the side. Running consists of a series of leaps or hops, and if the child has been well drilled in the fourth exercise of the alphabet, the fifth will be easier.

How to sit: Pupils occupy two positions at the desk, namely, "attention" and "rest." The first consists of sitting upright, the back free from the desk or chair, the chest arched, the head erect, the hands clasped and resting on the desk. The second, or "rest," permits the pupil to sit at ease in any good position of rest, to lean against the back of the desk, and to let the hands rest in the lap.

The reader is referred to the admirable work of Dr. Eliza M. Mosher, of Brooklyn, N. Y., on "The Posture of School Children." The command is, "Scholars, attention," or, "Scholars, rest."

CHAPTER XIV.

THE VOICE.—COMMANDS.

A CRITICISM frequently made by people who are competent to express their views on the subject, is this: many of the young men and young women who teach gymnastics do not know how to give commands. They do not understand how to use the voice in teaching. The speaking voice is pleasing, soft, and all that can be desired; but these are not the qualities for commanding a class. Much depends upon the manner in which the tone is made. The short, sharp, quick, decisive word which starts a class at once need not be cross or unkind; it is better than the sleepy command which fails to "stir" the pupils.

The question has been asked: "Can I, with my naturally weak voice, acquire the penetrating power that will be of service to me when I stand before a large number of pupils?" Yes, you can educate the voice, you can so train it that, when before your scholars, it will possess the desirable qualities. The teacher's natural voice may be shrill, which is unpleasant; and, while it may be deepened a few tones in speaking and commanding, it stops at a certain register. I should advise the teacher, therefore, to practice the commands daily. Every teacher should follow the advice of Comenius and "learn by doing." Each day something new is acquired by teaching. When walking along the streets, going home or coming back to the gymnasium, she should say over to herself one command, until perfectly learned. Not only repeat the command, but associate with the words the results. Let us take, for example, the command, "To the rear, *march!*" Repeat these words until it is understood which part of the command is *preparation* and which *execution*, remembering that there are two parts to every command : the first, which is called the preparatory command, such as, "To the rear" ; the second, which is the command of execution, such as the word *march*. Associate this command with some one walking along the street, and say, "To the rear, *march!* To the rear, *march!*" understanding that the word *march* must be given as the right foot comes to the ground. In the gymnasium it is advisable for the teacher to give commands to pupils who are stationed at the further part of the room. It is also a good plan to have the scholars stand with their backs to the teacher, when she is giving commands. Frequently when the teacher faces the class, the meaning is made evident by some motion of the arm or hand. If, however, she stands so that the class cannot see her, the clearness of the commands is tested.

The voice must be animated, clear, distinct. The commands should be given slowly at first, until the teacher can pronounce every part of the word and utter clearly every syllable. Later on the commands can be given very rapidly.

If the voice is weak, how can we train it? One method is by pronouncing the vowels *a, e, ä,* and *o;*

then pronouncing the word *ha*, or *haw*, until there is sufficient force back of the letter *h* to carry the voice to all parts of the room. The face is raised; do not give commands with the head forward. Rather aim the voice above the heads of the class so that, like a ball from a gun, it will ascend and go beyond them. If able to play a few chords on the piano, the teacher should practice singing the vowels until she can make the tones in the front part of the mouth; or, as one of our German teachers of singing has expressed it, "beyond the lips." When she has acquired this art she will know it, but until then the voice has a muffled sound, is back in the throat, tires her, and is disagreeable to the scholars. Possibly the reader may recall the sing-song tones of some school-teacher, as she called the children to the blackboard or drilled them in the three R's—the tiresome, monotonous, high-keyed voice that was exasperating. It is heard in too many schools to-day. It irritates the pupils. We too often find this voice in the gymnasium.

The voice for speaking and singing is different from that which is educated to give orders. The voice is one of the important mediums of transferring our wishes and our desires to the members of the class. When beginning to teach gymnastics the instructor will have to use the voice from one to four hours daily. If she has properly exercised vocal cords, the voice will not be greatly fatigued. With practice the voice can be used six or seven hours daily. The principal of a state normal school in Connecticut said: "I would rather you would spend more time drilling my girls in giving commands and in using their voices, than to put aside so much time for the gymnastic exercises. The gymnastic lesson, such as we shall give in the schoolroom, is easily learned, but the commands are not. We find that our teachers do not know how to describe the exercises and associate them with the wording of orders."

In our American system of gymnastics there is no nomenclature. One teacher gives one command to produce a stated result, another gives another command to produce the same result. The Germans have names or terms which are known to all the members of the North American Turn Bund. The German teacher from New York City can go to San Francisco, New Orleans, St. Louis, or Chicago, where he will find his commands obeyed immediately. They are already known; one command means one thing. The Swedes have a system of commands that is universal. The Americans have not.

We must pay more attention to the voices, and make a study of the nomenclature used in gymnastics. I shall never forget the lesson learned from one of my first teachers, Mr. R. J. Roberts, of the Young Men's Christian Association in Boston. He had a fine, clear voice, so full of enthusiasm and energy that it inspired the boys. They worked with a will and pleasure that were noticeable. Much of Mr. Roberts' success with young men was due to his voice. Nearly twenty years have passed since then, but the lesson was well learned and will not be forgotten, and I shall take pleasure in thanking Mr. Roberts for the help he gave me in this direction. The gymnastic instructor who possesses a poor voice should take a few lessons in singing, she should practice reading aloud, speaking slowly and very distinctly, should take every opportunity to strengthen and purify the tones when giving commands. This can be done at every lesson. Make a note of the words that are hard to pronounce. Do not spend too much time on the orders you can give well; they are cared for. Drill your pupils in counting aloud and count with them. Work with and without music. To drill a class with piano accompaniment requires a strong voice. Let part of the class sing while the rest exercise, and sing with them.

If a great part of the success of a teacher is due to the voice itself, much depends on the method of giving the command. The teacher must remember that it is harder to teach an exercise not shown, but described. She should therefore take pains to make her commands so clear that they will be easily understood. To do this the command must be a short one, the wording must be simple. If the command is a new one there should be a short period between the explanation and the word of execution, during which time the class thinks. All exercises should commence with the word *begin*, and be stopped by the word *halt*. After a command has been explained the teacher can say, "Ready, *begin!*" This allows more time.

When giving the commands for a compound exercise, part of which is new, comparatively new, or difficult, go rapidly over the exercises that are automatic, because they are controlled by the nerve centers; but very slowly over the motions that are new, or not so well learned.

THE VOICE.—COMMANDS. 169

This is perhaps a fine point in teaching, but it is worth considering. The teacher wishes to give the exercise shown in Fig. 15, which consists of swinging the right arm out, the left arm front, turning the face to the left, and a reverse charge with the right leg to the front. The easy exercises are swinging the arms and turning the head. The difficult part (we do not say it is new) is the reverse charge. The command is, "On the count one take a reverse charge with the right foot to the front; at the same time swing the right arm out, the left arm front, and turn the head to the left. Ready, One!" A study of the exercise or posture shows that the arms, head, and leg go in different directions, which is harder than having all go in the same direction. Four members of the body move at once, which is a more complicated exercise than using one member. Three of the movements are easy, one is hard. The movement of the head or either arm is automatic, but the combination of arm and head movements in different directions is not. Therefore the command must be so given that this will be made plain to the pupil. The charging motion is a reverse one. The direction associated with the right foot is to the right; we want the foot to go to the front. Therefore the command will thus be emphasized: "On the count *one* take a *reverse* charge with the *right* leg to the *front* (short pause), at the same time swing the *right* arm out (pause), the *left* arm *front* (pause), and turn the face to the *left*. *Ready* (pause), ONE!" It is more than likely that the majority will take the posture correctly.

When giving commands it is imperative that certain

words be emphasized. The emphasis must be on work that is not automatic. There should be pauses, not too long, that the pupil may grasp the idea. The command should not be too long, else the pupil forgets. It should not be too short, as it may not be explicit. Remember this rule: *Make the commands simple and clear*, as the class does an exercise according to its interpretation of the teacher's words.

Few, very few teachers make a study of the wording of a command, but all admit that commands are necessary, and all give them, but all do not get the same results. One teacher says *turn*, another *twist;* one says *flex* and *extend*, another *bend* and *straighten*. *Circling* and *swinging* are not synonymous. The first applies to all circles made with clubs or bells, the second to the pendulum motion of arms or legs. *Foot placing* and *foot stepping* are often applied to the same exercise. *Step the right foot forward*, and *take one step forward with the right foot* are not the same, but are frequently used by teachers in either sense. If instructors will be careful about not expressing commands in several different ways to produce one and the same result, we shall soon have a start made to establish a nomenclature in American gymnastics.

CHAPTER XV.

HINTS ON TEACHING A CLASS OF BOYS.

"A BOY," says Plato, " is the most vicious of all wild beasts." It is true that they are hard to manage in the gymnasium, not because they are naturally vicious or bad, but because of the surplus of animal spirits which keeps them in constant motion. The teacher must remember that it is well for the boy to dispose of this "animal life," and that by switching it in the right direction she can turn it to good account, thus preventing the disorder and unpleasantness which will surely arise if the teacher does not understand boy nature. It requires an artist to teach a child, but it requires an artist and a master to teach a boy. Some of the essential features of successful teaching are these :

In the first place, boys must be kept busy from the time they enter the gymnasium until they leave it. Again, they must be kept interested in the lesson. No teacher can successfully conduct a class of this character if the boys dislike the work. The result is too well known, the harsh, imperative commands, the driving of the boys, as one would drive animals with a whip, the incessant threats, the confusion, the general dissatisfaction. Interest, therefore, is an important feature.

The boys must be kept in order. The question arises now, What is meant by order in a boys' class? perfect silence, no whispering, no movement of the body? No. Nothing is gained by compelling the boys to maintain perfect silence. They cannot be kept perfectly still, therefore allow them to whisper, and during the short intervals of rest allow them to converse with each other and to move around some. The class in light gymnastics, of course, is kept busy, and will not have the opportunity to converse or to make bodily movements other than those which are given by the teacher. In heavy gymnastics, however, it is different. Here the boys must wait while the rest of the class are taking their turns on the bars, bucks, or rings. The busy boy is well looked after; the one who is at leisure is not. He will therefore amuse himself by striking, pushing, or pulling his companions, by leaving the ranks, climbing the ropes, jumping on other pieces of apparatus, or playing with the chest weights. This, of course, must not be tolerated. Let the boys laugh and talk, but not shout; allow them some latitude, but under no circumstances permit a boy to leave the ranks and touch another piece of apparatus.

I will digress at this point long enough to say that if a certain hour is set aside for the gymnastic training of a boy, he should not be allowed to go on the floor before that time nor to remain after the lesson is finished. If the teacher allows the boys to violate this rule and to play on the gymnasium floor, then he should at least see that all apparatus is pulled out of their reach and that they are not permitted to lower it.

Discipline forms an important part of a boy's training. Make few rules, but enforce them. The boy will very soon know whether the teacher intends to do this, and he will obey them or disobey them according to his opinion of the teacher. If a rule is made, it must be enforced. The first boy who violates it must meet with prompt and speedy punishment. There can be no dillydallying, delaying, or apologizing. Spencer has said that the boy who picks up a hot coal will be burned; the second time he picks up a coal he will be burned; the third time he attempts to do this he will be burned. Let the teacher of gymnastics learn from this. A boy violates a law, he is punished; he violates it a second time, he is punished. The third time he knows better, and he forms a better opinion of the teacher, he likes him better, and the parents are satisfied.

There is nothing that will cause disorder quicker than poor discipline. Many teachers are afraid of certain boys. They are not willing to incur the wrath or displeasure of the parents, or they know that such and such a boy is the son of one of the trustees, the principal of the school, or some man of prominence in the community. They are afraid to punish these boys. This of course will not do. Any boy, regardless of name and position, must expect to suffer the penalty of violating a law. It has been my pleasure to teach boys for nearly fifteen years, and I have yet to have any serious trouble with such parents, if I punished their boys. I have found that, in the majority of cases, the boy who is punished for wrong-doing does not complain at home. Only that one who has been wrongly punished will complain, and of course he has a right to do so. In such a case it is the duty of the teacher to settle the matter rightly. The instructor in gymnastics who makes a mistake will, at times, be obliged to acknowledge it. If he does not he loses prestige with the class.

The advice given by McLaren, in his work on heavy gymnastics, is good : Do not attempt to have perfect discipline from boys in heavy gymnastics, but approach as near as possible this ideal when teaching light work. Make allowance for the animal spirits and the life of your boys.

We all have to deal with the bad boy in the class. He is found everywhere. He is unruly at home, mischievous in school, mean with the other boys. It is not wise to spend too much time with this boy before the other members of the class. Let him understand at the start that you will not be trifled with, and that you do not intend to keep the other members of the class waiting while you punish him. It is not wise for you to lose your temper and scold the entire class just to punish one boy. It seems cowardly. An angry teacher cannot control boys. Do not, therefore, lose your temper with this refractory lad, but send him at once to his home, or to your office, and deal with him after the rest of the boys have gone. It is often the case that the boys themselves will punish such a comrade by their general opinion of him.

Do not give to your boys too much light work. Have you ever watched a number of children when they were allowed to enter a gymnasium for the first time? If you have not I should advise you to do so, and learn from your own observation. What do they do at first? The boys rush for the ropes, they climb upon the ladders, they put their legs through the rings, swing on the trapeze, jump over the sticks, "shin up" the poles.

What lesson are we to learn from this? That the interesting part of the gymnasium to these children—and I include under this head both boys and girls—is the heavy apparatus. They are fond of climbing, swinging, jumping, and leaping, but they do not like free and light gymnastics. I should therefore give to my classes plenty of heavy work, and should include in the lesson games and contests. One successful teacher of boys said that he knew "the nature of the beasts," and that he was successful because he compelled them to use their own energies, and he took advantage of their own desires. If play is the strong, the controlling passion of a child, then turn it to use in the gymnasium. The teacher must have a method, must follow out certain plans. There must be progression. No teacher of gymnastics should keep the class at the same work day after day. They must advance. This is especially true in free work. I have often told my boys that it was necessary for them to take a certain amount of medicine in the gymnasium, have made some fun of the light work, and we have gone through this part of the lesson, arousing a certain amount of interest.

You can keep the attention of a class of this kind by frequently giving them a lesson in "developing work." Take for the subject of a lesson the muscles of the arms, allow them to use light iron dumb bells, or take the one-pound wooden bell, and give each exercise from twenty to fifty times. There is no reason why we should give an exercise eight or sixteen times except that, in the case of piano accompaniment, it is better to make the changes at the end of a measure. In developing work do not always use the music. Give a certain number of movements for the biceps, then for the triceps. Exercises are taken for the front and the back of the forearm. Frequently at the close of the lesson measurements of the arms are taken, and the boys are greatly interested in the little increase they have made.

Fun is a good weapon to make use of in teaching boys. Make the lesson lively, start the pupils laughing. A good joke does no harm. Boys are greatly interested in what the college men do, and it is well for the teacher to become acquainted with college methods and to give the series of exercises that are used by the members of the crew, the nine, and the teams.

The teacher must be on the lookout for the timid boy. He will hold back from jumping exercises, he will drop out of the contests, he will hide rather than do the high jumping. He is afraid of his comrades, and shrinks from their laughter. This child should be dealt with, if the teacher has time, at the close of the lesson. By taking him apart from the rest, he can be taught to jump over the stick, to take a standing broad jump, and perhaps to hang by his knees on the bar. All boys are not alike, and the lesson cannot be likened to a coat that will fit each member of the class.

The reckless boy must be held in check. He is found wherever the boys congregate.. He will do just a little more than any one else; he climbs higher, he tries to jump farther, he does many tricks that are dangerous. He should be repressed.

There is the fat boy, who is the butt of the class. They laugh at his attempts, they find much merriment in his failure to execute the tricks. He laughs with them, but in the majority of cases he feels it, and you will notice that this boy will, sooner or later, drop out of the class, and the parents will complain that you have allowed the other boys to make fun of him. Under no conditions allow the boys to make fun of any one. A certain amount of laughter is tolerated when a boy makes a mistake, but the guying and, as the college men say, the "horsing" of any boy must not be tolerated.

Look out for accidents. They are apt to happen during the periods of "break ranks" and rest. They are sure to occur if the scholars are allowed to go on to the floor before the class begins or if they are permitted to remain at the close of the lesson. An accident reflects discredit upon the teacher, whether he is to blame or not, and the parents or guardians lay this up against the gymnasium. The teacher, of course, has in his office the necessary bandages for binding up arms. If he is a physician he can look after the bruises. If he is not, it is well for him to have taken some work in emergencies, that he may prepare the case for the physician.

The teacher should be careful about giving "break ranks" too frequently. This division of the hour is a good one: the class is called into line and receives a short drill in military work; but it is not wise to give instruction in this line of gymnastics unless military discipline accompanies the teaching. Do not try to teach forming twos and fours, or marching four or five abreast, unless the order is good. Single file marching,

marching on tiptoes or on the heels, some drills in facings—this simple work can be given.*

Free gymnastics should be given at each lesson. The teacher should make a point of dealing with the most common physical defects. While it is well for the exercises to be arranged according to the laws of Ling, if the time is short there can be changes made in the day's order. The boys should be drilled at every lesson in exercises for widening and deepening the chest, increasing the capacity of the lungs, and strengthening the action of the heart. There should be precipitant or running work given, and certain drills for developing the muscles along the spine.

After the free work, a few minutes should be set aside for a drill in light gymnastic exercises with the bells or wands, this to be followed by the regular drill in heavy work, and the lesson to close with a jump or a game.

If the hour were to be divided into minutes we would arrange the lesson about as follows :

Military work, about 8 minutes.

Rest, 2 minutes.

Free work, corrective work, and running, 10 minutes.

Rest, 3 minutes.

Light gymnastics, bells, wands, or clubs, 10 minutes.

Rest, 3 minutes.

Heavy gymnastics and the game, the rest of the hour.

See that the boys go directly to the dressing room when the class is dismissed, that they take their baths, dress quietly, and leave the building. Do not allow the

---

* The author has planned lessons for a boys' class for one year which can be obtained at the Yale Gymnasium.

crowd of boys to go rushing pellmell to the dressing room, take their time putting on their clothing, and go home when they please. Give them from fifteen to twenty minutes to go to the dressing room, make the necessary changes, do what bathing they are allowed to do, and leave the building. The boy who remains after this time should be carefully questioned. If it is found that his clothing has been tied in a knot, that his shoes have been taken away, or that he has lost anything, request him in the future to report any loss, that assistance may be given him. If he had no good reason for remaining beyond the twenty minutes, punish him— the first time by a reprimand, the second time by the loss of the lesson. A reliable monitor should be stationed in the dressing room if the teacher does not go with the boys, but he certainly should accompany them.

One unpleasant element in the handling of boys is their yelling when allowed to leave the classroom and go to the baths. They should be warned beforehand, and if they violate the rule the class should be punished—in which case the innocent will suffer with the guilty, but we cannot at first tell which boys caused the trouble. The honest boys would tell the truth and be punished for their honesty, while those who would lie about it would go free, and be rewarded for dishonesty. By punishing the entire class—which may be preventing their doing the work which they most liked at the next lesson—the yelling would very soon stop, and the boys who were not to blame would settle the question with those who were. If it is true, and we know it is, that boys are fond of yelling, give them a drill in counting aloud and let them have a class yell, or work them with so much ardor that they will not feel like indulging in this form of fun after they have finished their lesson.

There will be some stealing going on in the gymnasium. The teacher should request the boys to leave their money and valuables in the office. Keys to the lockers will be lost, shoes and stockings will be taken, costumes will be missing; but these are some of the thorns which prick the flesh of our instructors in gymnastics. We must expect them. We must use a great deal of care in dealing with a case of theft. The best way to prevent things of this kind is for the teacher to be with the boys when they come to the gymnasium, while they are exercising, and remain with them until they leave.

One word about the class falling in or taking footmarks. A bell can be rung, and the scholars should be given from fifteen to sixty seconds to take their places on the floor. It is well for the teacher to notice, before the bell is rung, that the boys are not too high up on the ladders, or up in the rafters of the building, so that in their hurry to take their places they will not fall. Then he can wait the allotted number of seconds after the bell has rung, when the boy who has not reported or who is late must be called to account. Otherwise several commands are given for the class to fall in, a great deal of shouting is indulged in, the bell is rung so many times that it loses its value. The bell should be rung but *once;* the teacher waits a certain number of seconds; those who are late are punished. The question is very soon settled; the boys soon learn to respond rapidly. If these rules are enforced strictly the first day, they must be enforced the second day; at no time can the teacher be lax.

Interest has been aroused by placing in the gymnasium a bulletin board, upon which we put the names of the boys and the records they make. We organize, in nearly every case, a gymnasium society. A president, vice-president, secretary, and treasurer are elected, also a captain of the teams. The secretary keeps the names of the boys, the record of their strength tests, their height, weight, and lung capacity—keeping only a few, not many. The boys are allowed to test their lungs perhaps once a week; we see and note the number of times they can dip on the bars or pull up on the horizontal bar, and the record is kept. This is a simple means of arousing and maintaining interest.

It will be found that a certain number of boys cut their lessons, especially the first part; they will come in late to the class. The boys who do this should be excused from the interesting part of the work. They will in future report in time for that part of the hour which is not interesting to them, viz.: light work. The teacher must remember that the boy should have an opportunity to give reasons, and the teacher acts as the judge and settles the questions.

Give talks on health and morals, tell stories while the boys are seated on the floor, or it may be that once in a while they can be called together in some recitation room for this purpose.

I do not believe that women should teach heavy gymnastics to boys. It is better that a man take charge of this work. The reason is plain. Boys respect those who can do better work than they can. The teacher is severely criticised by the members of the boys' class if it is found that he or she cannot do the work upon the bars or upon the ticks that some of the boys in the class can do. It is galling to the teacher, and not pleasant for the class.

The teacher must overlook some things. It is not always wise to stir up the small gossip which is found in a boys' class, nor wise to make a great ado about nothing.

The best way to handle boys is by kindness. Threaten as little as possible.

The teacher should observe the faces of the boys, and in case any one shows great fatigue, the face is pale, the breathing irregular, or the child places the hand upon the side, showing that there is pain, this boy must be looked after, the heart examined, the lungs tested, or he should be allowed to go to the office and rest. Remember that the small boys will work as hard as they can to keep up with big boys, that the weak will do, or try to do, the work of the strong.

Avoid being partial. Look out for favoritism. Once in a while a question box can be placed in the gymnasium and the boys allowed to write questions and place them here. These are to be answered either by the teacher or by some member of the class. Whistling is given to the class frequently, also singing. Rope splicing is taught if the class is small and the time will permit. I urge the teacher to make a study of books that will be interesting to boys.

CHAPTER XVI.

MILITARY GYMNASTICS.

THE chapter devoted to this subject will contain suggestions for the beginner, yet it may be that those who have had many years' experience will find hints that will be helpful.

Only a few of the maneuvers have been described, but by studying these the observant teacher will be able to apply the principles to the more intricate evolutions. The text is taken from both the old and new tactics, but is frequently modified from the requirements of soldiers to those of pupils. The descriptions are for single ranks only. The teacher who wishes to know more of military work than is described here will find in the book entitled "Light Gymnastics," by the same author, a series of illustrated marching movements.

The position of attention. An analysis of the position of a soldier will draw our attention to thirteen points, with all of which the instructor should be familiar. The question "Why?" is so frequently asked that it is at times embarrassing to the teacher if she has not given sufficient study to the subject to answer readily. The description of this position, taken from Upton, is:

Heels on the same line, as near to each other as the conformation of the body will permit.

The feet turned out equally, forming with each other an angle of about sixty degrees.

Knees straight, without stiffness of body.

The body erect on the hips, inclining a little forward.

Shoulders square, and falling equally.

Arms hanging naturally.

Elbows near the body.

Fingers closed and extended, thumb along the first finger.

Palms of the hands turned slightly to the front.

Little finger behind the seam of the trousers.

Head erect and to the front.

Chin slightly drawn in, without constraint.

Eyes straight to the front, and striking the ground at about the distance of fifteen yards.

The new tactics have modified this arrangement, and give for the position of a soldier the following rules :

Heels on the same line, and as near each other as the conformation of the man permits.

Feet turned out equally and forming with each other an angle of about sixty degrees.

Knees straight, without stiffness.

Body erect on the hips, inclining a little forward; shoulders square, and falling equally.

Arms and hands hanging naturally, backs of the hands outward ; little fingers opposite the seams of the trousers ; elbows near the body.

Head erect and square to the front ; chin slightly drawn in, without constraint; eyes straight to the front.

The Swedish position of attention, or, as it is termed, the fundamental standing position, is this:

Heels together or slightly apart.
Feet at an angle of ninety degrees.
Knees straight.
Hips carried backward.
Chest forward and well expanded.
Shoulders held back and down.
Head erect.
Chin drawn in.
Arms along the sides.
Palms flat, on the outside of the thighs, and drawn slightly backward.
Weight of the body carried well forward.*

In the main points the Swedish, German, and American fundamental standing positions are similar. They vary principally in detail. It is not our intention so much to discuss the merits of the position, but rather how we shall teach it. While at times we may digress, and speak of the comparative merits of this or that exercise or position, we shall try to explain the best method of presenting the subject, this being more the object of the book.

In the first place, it is easy to commence the description of the position by beginning at the bottom and describing the angle of the feet. With us it is about sixty degrees. I know of no serious objection to ninety degrees, but think that the small angle is the more natural one. A basic attitude of ninety degrees is stronger than one only two thirds this size. It is easier to approximate the

---
* Posse's "Handbook of School Gymnastics."

larger base, because a right angle is formed. The heels should touch, if the calves of the legs are not too large, or the child not knock-kneed.

Pass from the feet to the knees, which are held as close together as the conformation of the body will permit. It may be well to warn young teachers about criticising pupils for not touching their knees, when they (the pupils) are bow-legged. Scholars who have this defect are apt to be sensitive about it, although one small boy remarked, when the teacher criticised him, that "his knees were not on speaking terms." Professor Brosius, a very prominent German teacher of gymnastics, said that it was possible to overcome this defect by the use of will power, and that he had in his classes young men who had been able to bring their knees together by holding the correct standing position. An exaggerated movement of the hips backward will sometimes assist the scholar in touching the knees. If the bow in the leg extends from the knee to the ankle, it is, of course, a different matter.

Pass from the knees to the hips, which should be forced back, and from this part of the body to the chest, which should be well arched. By giving these two commands and insisting upon their being obeyed, we do away with having to call attention to the prominent abdomen.

Next the shoulders engage our attention. They are level, and well drawn back. Some teachers object to using the two terms, "arch the chest" and "draw the shoulders back," claiming that one cannot be done without the other. It is not an important point to discuss. By calling attention to the two parts of the body additional emphasis is laid on the description.

The arms should hang naturally at the side, with the elbows somewhat back. The hand is in what is termed the fundamental position, viz.: fingers close and extended, thumb along the first finger. The position of the hand may be taught before beginning with any other part of the body.

The head is erect, the eyes to the front. Call attention to the fact that if the eyes are cast down the head drops forward. For the same reason, do not allow the child to look up, because the head will be elevated and the chin will protrude. Consequently we say the eyes should be cast upon the ground fifteen yards to the front. It is, perhaps, clearer to say to the pupil, "Look straight ahead." According to the directions given, the chin is slightly drawn in.

We have now finished the parts of the body; let us take it as a whole. The weight is inclined somewhat forward on the balls of the feet. This enables the pupil to start off promptly. At the same time the fore part of the feet form a more springy base than the heels. (See Fig. 8.)

The teacher will notice that we began this description at the feet and went up to the head, taking the parts in turn. This method of teaching is not, of course, so good for children, who are too young to appreciate the details. A child in normal physical condition naturally stands well. Children are taught by the picture method, so by referring to soldiers and asking them to stand as they do, we get better results than from a description, which is almost meaningless to them. Very frequently the teacher may obtain good results by calling to the platform a well-built boy or girl, and showing the class what is meant by the proper standing position. At the same time she can have the child stand against the measuring pole, to show how easy it is for them to keep the head, shoulders, hips, calves, and heels in a straight line.

The position of attention is the first thing we teach to classes. It is important, and the instructor should impress it upon the pupils that they should not only learn to hold the body well, but should always keep it so while in the gymnasium (or out of it), and they should associate this carriage of the body with the gymnasium.

Let us now consider the next step in teaching military work. It will be the rest which follows the constrained position of attention. The command is, "Company in place, *rest!*" The new tactics give it, "Company, at ease!" The former command is preferable. At the word of execution, the pupil is allowed at first to stand upon either foot, taking the position natural for him. This will give the teacher an opportunity to observe the easy standing position of the pupils. The position of "place rest," advocated by Dr. Eliza Mosher of Brooklyn, N. Y., in her paper entitled "The Influence of the Habitual Posture on the Symmetry and Health of the Body," should be known by all gymnastic teachers. (Fig. 16.)

Scholars who are in the habit of carrying the weight upon the right foot when resting should change, and allow the weight to rest upon the other.

Facings. We use under this heading, right or left,

Fig. 14.—Foot Placing, One Foot Length. (Page 161.)

Fig. 15.—Right Arm Out, Left Arm Front, Face to Left, Reverse Charge, Left Leg Front. (Page 169.)

In Place Rest. (Page 188.)

right or left oblique, and right or left about face. The facings seem so simple, are apparently so easy to execute, and are used so frequently, that little importance is attached, not only to their being accurately done, but to being correctly taught. Here, as elsewhere, the haste that marks our teaching crops out, and the result is obvious. The teacher who neglects the rudiments of military drill will suffer for her carelessness. She will lose many minutes, later in the season, finding fault with the class for doing poor work, when she herself is to blame. Therefore spend time teaching a class to face, first to the right and then to the left, next half face to the right and the left, or, as it is termed, right oblique or left face. Although it seems, according to the sequence of movements, that the oblique should be taught before the full right or left face, it is customary to teach the ninety degree turn first. Not enough time is spent in teaching the oblique facings; consequently, when marching in single file and the command is given, "Column half right (or left), *march!*" it will be noticed that the scholars do not clearly understand the movement, nor do they execute it well.

I have taught, and shall continue to teach, the facings in this manner: With the body as one piece, turn forty-five degrees or a right oblique, ninety degrees or a right face, one hundred and eighty degrees or a right about face, on the left heel. The turns to the left are to be made upon the same heel. This simplifies the work. The question arises at once, Why not use the Swedish facing, or that found in the new tactics? My answer is, the former is very simple, easily learned, and long remembered. I have not found it so with the other facings. It is essential that the body be well balanced and smartly turned. Avoid facing on what is sometimes termed the instalment plan—the head going first, the shoulders next, etc.

The facing, as described by Upton, is as follows: To the right or left, command, "Right (or left), *face!*" At the command *face*, raise the right foot slightly, face to the right, turning on the left heel, the left toe slightly raised; replace the right heel by the side of the left and on the same line. The facings to the left are executed upon the same heel as the facings to the right.

The right face, as given in the new tactics, is thus described: Command, "Right, *face!*" Raise slightly the right heel and left toe and face to the right, turning on the left heel, assisted by a slight pressure on the ball of the right foot; replace the right foot.

There is little in this method of facing to the right to commend it. It is awkward, hard to teach, difficult to learn, and not more sure to produce an accurate turn of the body than the old facing. I prefer the Swedish plan, in spite of the argument brought against it, that the entire body is shifted out of place by the latter facing. In a short conversation with a well-known West Point man, he expressed the opinion that the facing to the right, as given in the new tactics, was not satisfactory.

The Swedish facing is: To face to the flank, command, "Right, *face!*" The pupil turns on his right heel ninety degrees to the right and supports the motion by the ball of the left foot; when this is done he replaces his left foot beside the right one in fundamental position. Facing to the right is done on the right heel, to the left on the left.

The teacher, of course, chooses the plan that best suits him. It is not so much which method he adopts, but how he teaches it. The about facing is very confusing to the pupil who tries to remember the different ways. For example, there is the about face of the common soldier as distinguished from that of the officer; there are the Swedish, German, and the new tactics about face, in all five kinds.

To the rear. Command, "About, *face!*" At the command *about*, turn on the left heel, bring the left toe to the front, carry the right foot to the rear, the hollow opposite to and three inches from the left heel, the feet square to each other. At the command *face*, turn on both heels, raise the toes a little, face to the rear, and when the face is nearly completed raise the right foot and replace it by the side of the left. (Old tactics.)

To the rear. Command, "About, *face!*" Raise slightly the left heel and right toe, face to the rear, turning to the right on the right heel and the ball of the left foot; replace the left foot beside the right. (New tactics.)

Why bother the teacher or pupils with so many terms? I do not like the old tactics face for the soldier, as it is hard to teach and remember, and too complicated. The new tactics and Swedish about face are similar, and both are good; the about face of the officer is an accurate and a graceful one; but the simplest of all, to my mind, is the German method. There is truth in the argument that one is apt to lose his balance, but I have not found that the pupil is long bothered by this trouble.

The teacher must not attempt to teach any facing movement, or illustrate it, without having practiced it carefully before a looking glass, if this is possible.

Marking time. Being in march. Command, "Mark time, *march!*" At the command *march*, given as either foot is coming to the ground, continue the cadence and make a semblance of marching, without gaining ground, by alternately advancing each foot about half its length, and bringing it back on a line with the other.

It is not hard to teach marking time, consequently but little space will be given to this subject. Our explanation of the method of teaching is this: Notice that the left foot moves first, not only in marking time, but also in marching. Therefore by your drill impress this on the minds of the pupils, so that the movement will become automatic. This may be done in several ways, one of which is to permit the scholar to first stamp lightly with the left foot, next to tap the floor with the ball of the same foot, then to swing the left foot forward one half its length, and finally to teach the regular method. The teacher must call attention to the distance allowed for swinging the foot, otherwise the pupils will soon throw the foot forward more than half its length. Analysis of marking time shows that, at the preliminary command, "Company, mark time!" the pupil transfers the weight to the right foot. This slight motion of the body is an important feature of the drill. When the command of execution, *Mark!* or, as the tactics give it, *March!* is given, the left knee is slightly bent, the heel is lifted from the floor, the thigh is sufficiently flexed to permit the leg to swing forward a short distance. At the finish the foot falls back to position, the weight is transferred, and the same operation is gone through with the other leg. Attention is called to the knee bending, that the teacher may know how to prevent the stiff leg marking time. We can tell by the action of the heads whether the members of the class are marking time in unison.

The Germans, when marking time, accent the movement, extending the foot forward and downward, pointing with the toes. The teacher may have noticed that, when the scholars take an exercise that is noisy, such as stamping the foot or slapping the hands, they work more in unison than when executing a movement in silence. Therefore, make use of this, and begin marking time by making a noise, as stamping the foot. This method is used not only for children, but even for adults. I have often had more difficulty in instructing a class of teachers to mark time than children, but the principles of teaching a child are good for adults too.

The start. The start, in marching, must receive attention, as the relative position of the files and the evenness of the lines depend, to some extent, upon it. It is better, therefore, to drill the pupils when standing in a line, *i. e.*, side by side, than when in a file, one back of the other. Use the new tactics so far as possible, when drilling a line; that is, allow six or eight inches between persons. This may be secured by permitting them to place the left hand on the hip. (See aligning and falling in.) The command may be given, "Company, forward, *march!*" At the command *forward*, the pupils transfer the weight to the right foot and incline the body forward. Drill the class in this movement several times, bringing them back to the fundamental standing position, or attention, by the command, "As you were." At the command *march*, the pupil steps off briskly with the left foot, taking a natural length step. It is of little use to tell the members of a class to step twenty or twenty-five inches. Point or aim the body at a certain point on the opposite wall, and march in a direct line to the front. The step should be even and the cadence regular. In our marching, we take about 65 steps a minute for common time, 90 steps for quick time, 48 for slow, and from 120 to 180 for double time.

The halt. The command *halt* is given at the discretion of the teacher, who says, "Company, *halt!*" The command of execution is given as either foot comes to the floor, plant this foot, take one additional step, and bring the heels together. This allows them time to think, and the halt is made on the third count. Later the company can halt on one or two counts. The halt from marking time is generally made, during the early teaching, in two counts after the command; thus, "Company, halt, one, two!" Finally the halt can be made on one count. The pupils must be thoroughly drilled on the halt and on the start. Here, as before, we may make use of a noisy start and stop, permitting the pupils to stamp the left foot on the first step after the command, "Company, forward, *march!*" and to repeat the stamp on the last count after the command *halt*. This plan of teaching is used by both the Swedes and the Germans.

It is out of the question for a teacher to expect to have

a well-drilled class if she does not pay strict attention to these details. They are not always observed in our military companies, nor do pupils fancy them, but the choice is not to be left to the pupil. The start and halt in marching may be better taught and learned if the teacher will drill the class in taking first one, then two, and finally three or more steps, thus : The teacher after showing the exercise commands, "Class one step forward, counting aloud, *march!*" At the command *march*, the scholar advances the left foot and counts one; he brings the right foot alongside of the left, and counts two. Thus he has taken one step, but has counted two. In this way he will advance two steps and count three, or three steps and count four, there being one more count than step, the halt being made on the last count. In taking steps, the pupil advances first the left, and then the right foot.

An example of how to teach a step may be given here, and it will be of service to the new teacher. She says, "I want the members of the class to take one step forward, this way"; she shows the exercise. The picture has been drawn, and the class has a better idea of what the teacher wants them to do. She then says, "As you take the step forward, count, this way"; she again illustrates the movement and counts. By this time the dullest one in the class understands what is to be done. The teacher then says, "At the command *march*, take one step"; and in a firm, decided way she repeats the command and gives the word of execution. It has taken but a short time, the exercise has been carefully illustrated, and the movement should be well done.

Change step. Command, "Change step, *march!*" At the command *march*, given as the right foot comes to the ground, the left foot is advanced and planted; the toe of the right is then advanced near the heel of the left, the recruit again stepping off with the left. The change on the right foot is similarly executed, the command *march* being given as the left foot strikes the ground. (New tactics.)

The pupil will notice that the command is, "Change step, *march!*" I do not like the word *march*, but prefer to repeat the word *change*, as it produces the same result and is more closely associated with the movement than the word march.

We had in one of our military companies an officer who seemed to know Upton nearly by heart. He could give command after command without omitting a single word, his face was animated, his teaching full of life; but when the test came later in the season, and his men were drilled in the preliminary movements, it was found that they did not do the work so well as the soldiers taught by less brilliant officers. One fault was his rapid speaking, and the "parrot" fashion in which he gave the commands. He did not take enough time to explain the movements, he preferred to "rattle off" commands in his glib fashion, and he lost his patience when the soldiers were apparently dull. The fault, however, was his own, and it was due to this that, even in the teaching how to change step, he failed.

This is a difficult exercise to teach. It may be associated with another that will be given very soon, viz.: "To the rear, *march!*" Instructors seem to have as much trouble teaching these two maneuvers as any of the simple drills found in military work. There is a reason for this. The movement is hard to teach because the teacher confuses the right and the left foot. It is not easy to say the word *march* or *change* just before the right foot comes to the floor, immediately after which command the movement is executed, consequently there is little time in which to think. The command "Change step!" may be given at any time, but the final word of execution must be given at a certain time.

To teach successfully these seemingly simple exercises, the teacher should practice the movements before giving them to the class, in order that she may bring back to her own mind the teaching she received years before.

No command or movement can be well taught until it has been analyzed by the instructor. Changing step should be one of the first things taught in a school. If it is a difficult matter for an adult to learn this, how much harder will it be for a child, and yet few children keep step when taking their first lessons. I have never attempted to teach a child this movement as I should teach it to an adult. The method of instructing little ones is by first teaching them which is the left foot, then compelling them to stamp the left foot upon a certain count, and, without going into the details of the movement, I have found that they would in a short time change step, and do it correctly. Changing step is the same movement that a schoolgirl makes when she goes skipping along the sidewalk. It is the "hippety-hop" that children know so well. The movement may be more quickly learned by adults if they are permitted to take one half the movement a number of times in succession; *i. e.*, to slide the right foot forward, bring the left foot up to the heel of the right, step off again with the right, and so on. By doing this, they associate the special movement in changing step with the command.

The command *change* as the left foot comes to the floor is not often given.

Side step. Command, "Right (or left) step, *march!*" Carry the right foot twelve inches to the right, keeping knees straight and shoulders square to the front; as soon as the right foot is planted, bring the left foot to the side of it, and continue the movement, observing the cadence for each foot, as explained for quick time. The side step is not executed in double time. (New tactics.)

This is a simple drill, easily taught and soon learned. The only difficulty in teaching this is that the scholars slide the feet, which should not be allowed; they take steps that are too long. The command *halt* is given as one foot comes to the floor, the foot is planted and the other brought alongside (generally taken on one count). In class drills little is gained by giving quick time, therefore the side step is given in common time. Avoid the marking time movement of the foot in side step marching. Take this step.

Back step. Command, "Backward, *march!*" Step back with the left foot fifteen inches straight to the rear, measuring from heel to heel, then with the right, and so on, the feet alternating. At the command *halt*, bring back the foot in front to the side of the one in rear. The back step is used for short distances only and is not executed in double time.

The *short step, side step,* and *back step* may be executed from *mark time* and conversely.

The back step is an easy movement. There are no special rules for teaching it. It is well, however, to drill the class in halting from the backward march. It can be done in two counts.

To march to the rear. Being in march, the instructor commands, "To the rear, *march!*" At the command *march*, given as the right foot strikes the ground, advance and plant the left foot; then turn on the balls of both feet, face to the right about, and immediately step off with the left foot.

We have to teach what seems to be a simple exercise, and one which does not receive a great deal of attention in many of our military schools. There is a way, however, of teaching the movement that will be of assistance to the leader. In the first place, the step must be so well learned by the instructor, that when standing before a class it will be "second nature" to her. Here, as in changing step, the teacher will have some trouble in remembering the feet; that is, she will confuse the right and the left. The command "To the rear!" may be given at any time; the command *march* must be given as the right foot strikes the ground. This will permit the scholar to advance the left, during which short period he has an opportunity to think, then turn 180 degrees to the right, pivoting upon the balls of both feet, and start off in the new direction with the left foot.

It is a good plan for the teacher to watch people on the street and to repeat the command, always thinking the word *march* as the right foot comes to the ground. No one can instruct a class well who is obliged to think a great deal of her own work. Marching to the rear is more easily learned if the scholars are permitted to stamp the left foot after they have turned 180 degrees.

Double time. The length of the full step in double time is thirty-six inches; the cadence is at the rate of 180 steps per minute. To march in double time the command is, "Forward, double time, *march!*"

At the command *forward*, throw the weight of the body on the right leg; at the command *double time*, raise the hands until the forearms are horizontal, fingers closed, nails toward the body, elbows to the rear.

At the command *march*, carry forward the left foot, leg slightly bent, knee somewhat raised, and plant the foot thirty-six inches from the right; then execute the same motion with the right foot; continue this alternate movement of the feet, throwing the weight of the body forward and allowing a natural swinging motion to the arms. The pupils should also be exercised in running, the principles being the same as for double time.

When marching in double time and running, the pupils breathe as much as possible through the nose, keeping the mouth closed. (New tactics.)

Boys run better than girls. Women, as a rule, are not good runners. They keep the arms too still. The arms must swing to balance the body, and it is essential that the movements be free and elastic. Teach pupils to run lightly, quietly, and on tiptoes. One hundred and fifty, even two hundred steps, can be taken a minute. Drill the class frequently in running in place, the command being, "Company, in place, *run!*" at which time they will go through the running movement but do not gain ground. From this they can be given either the command, " Forward, *run !* " or, "Company, *halt !* " From running in place the halt is made in two counts. We do not often give the command *halt* from double time when the class is gaining ground, on account of the impetus given the body. It is preferable first to come to slow time. Do not touch the heels to the floor when running.

Alignments. The instructor first teaches the pupils to align themselves scholar by scholar, the better to comprehend the principles of alignments; to this end she advances the two scholars on the right three or more yards, and having aligned them, commands, "By file, right (or left), dress, *front !* "

At the command *dress*, the pupils move up successively in quick time, shortening the last step so as to find themselves about six inches behind the alignment. Each pupil then moves on the line, which must never be passed, taking steps of two or three inches, casting his eyes to the right so as to see the buttons on the coat of the pupil second from him, keeping his shoulders square to the front, and touching with his elbow that of the one next to him without opening his arms.

At the command *front*, given when the rank is well aligned, the pupils cast their eyes to the front and remain firm.

According to the old tactics, the scholars fall in at a right face, or one standing directly back of the other. This is done in order that new pupils may be easily placed in line, or, if changes are made, the file is not so apt to be disturbed as it would be if the pupils were standing side by side. While the pupils are standing at facing distance in single files, instruct them in dressing to the front. Facing distance, when in single file, is the length of the forearm from the one next in front, and is tested by flexing the forearm. (See Fig. 17.) It is well to associate the word *dress* with the "dressing down," or the planing of a board. Scholars are to be taught that, when the line is perfectly dressed, it is trim, neat, and straight. Give the command " Left, *face*," and teach right and left dressing.

The matter of aligning a class and dressing does not require a great deal of practice. The movements are easily taught and learned. There is one point, however, that will be of service to the teacher, *i. e.*, a rapid method of arranging scholars according to their height. It is possible to form a file in a short time if the instructor knows how. We generally ask our pupils to fall in in a file on one side of the room, according to their height, the shortest standing in front and the tallest at the rear. Pupils above a certain age are able to align themselves in a creditable manner. After "falling in," if the instructor stands at some little distance from the file, she will be able to tell at a glance whether this one or that one is too short, aligning by the heads, and not by the height of the shoulders. If a second alignment is to be made, have the shortest one take three steps to the left or right. The teacher can then indicate who should come next.

To march in a line. Being in line at a halt, command, "Forward, guide right (or left), *march!*" The pupils step off, the guide marching straight to the front. The instructor sees that the pupils preserve the interval toward the side of the guide; that they yield to pressure from that side and resist pressure from the opposite direction; that by slightly shortening or lengthening the step, they gradually recover the alignment, and by slightly opening out or closing in, they gradually recover the interval, if lost; that while habitually keeping the head to the front, they may occasionally glance toward the side of the guide to assure themselves of the alignment and interval, but that the head is turned as little as possible for this purpose. To change the guide, command, "Guide right (or left)." (New tactics.)

It is taken for granted that the teacher understands the difference between a file and a line. (See Terms.) Attention is called to the placing of guides when marching in a line. If the class is a small one, the guide can be placed upon the right or the left. If it is a large one, I prefer to place the guide in the center, in which case the command is, "Company, forward (or backward), guide center, *march!*"

To march by the flank. Being at a halt the instructor commands, "Right (or left), *face!* Forward, *march!*" If in march the instructor commands, "By the right (or left) flank, *march!*" At the command *march*, given as the right foot strikes the ground, advance and plant the left foot, then turn to the right and step off in the new direction with the right foot. In the march by the flank the scholars cover each other and keep closed to *facing distance*, that is, to such distance that in forming line the elbows will touch.

One who understands how to teach right and left face

will find no difficulty in having the class execute this movement when they are at a halt. But it requires some thought on the part of the instructor to give the command *march* when the class is in motion. The instructor should try this movement a number of times before taking the class, and should drill small rather than large squads.

The flank movement is used a great deal in our marching. The spectator is not aware that a mistake has been made in the facing if all the scholars turn about the same time, nor does it annoy the scholars, but it is well for them to be drilled in these movements, if time will allow and the discipline of the school will permit. It must be understood, however, that military work amounts to little if the teacher does not have military discipline. It seems almost impossible to secure this order in a number of our schools. When this is the case, reduce the military work to a minimum.

To change direction in column of files. The members of the class have been previously well drilled in right and left oblique facing, or half facing to the right and the left. An important point to remember is that the scholars must learn to march in a direct line to the front. In other words, they must "cover points," or aim the body at a certain point and walk toward that, regardless of where the one next in front goes. In "Column half right (or half left)," every member of the class must march to the given point and turn forty-five degrees, then march in the new direction. One reason why these simple movements are so poorly done is because the teacher passes rapidly over them, anxious to drill the class upon the more elaborate and showy exercises. No instructor can secure the best results who does not pay attention to detail training.

To oblique. Being in line at a halt, or marching, command, "Right (or left) oblique, *march!*" Each man half faces to the right, at the same time stepping off in the new direction. He preserves his relative position, keeping his shoulders parallel with those of the one next on his right, and so regulates his step as to make the head of this pupil conceal the heads of the others in the rank. At the command *halt*, the men halt, faced to the front. (New tactics.)

This maneuver will not be well done until the pupils have been thoroughly drilled in right and left oblique facing and marching in a direct line. To march in the oblique direction when in file is not so hard as to execute a similar movement when four or eight are abreast.

Wheelings. Wheeling on a fixed pivot. Being at a halt the instructor commands, "In circle right (or left) wheel, *march!*"

At the command *march* the pupils, except the pivot man, step off with the left foot, turning at the same time the head a little to the left, the eyes fixed on the line of the eyes of the men to their left; the pivot man marks time strictly in his place, gradually turning his body, to conform to the movement of the marching flank; the one who conducts this flank takes steps of twenty-eight inches, and, from the first step, advances the left shoulder a little, casts his eyes along the rank, and feels lightly the elbow of the next pupil toward the pivot, but never pushes him.

The others touch with the elbow toward the pivot, resist pressure from the opposite side, conform to the movement of the marching flank, and shorten their steps according to their distance from it. After wheeling around the circle several times the instructor commands, "*Halt!*"

Wheeling on a movable pivot. Being in march, to change direction the instructor commands, "Right (or left) wheel, *march*, forward, *march!*"

The first command is given when the squad is three yards from the wheeling point.

At the command *march*, the wheel is executed as on a fixed pivot, except that the pivot man, instead of turning in his place, takes steps of nine inches, and thus gains ground forward in describing a small curve so as to clear the wheeling-point.

The radius of the circle described by the pivot man increases with the size of the squad, and is equal to nearly one half of the front of the squad or subdivision.

Wheelings on fixed or movable pivot being important movements, the instructor requires the pupils successively to act as pivots and to conduct the marching flank.

The following simple rule for wheeling with three, four, five, or more abreast, will assist the instructor. If there are four abreast the pupils take only four steps to wheel ninety degrees, eight steps to wheel one hundred and eighty degrees, sixteen steps to wheel in a complete circle.

If there are five wheeling they take five steps to wheel ninety degrees. Six persons take six steps, and so on.

There is always one more count than the number of steps taken.

Illustration: In "Fours, right, *march*," the pupils will take only four steps, but will count five.

Wheelings. The first wheel is generally made when the scholars are marching around the room four abreast. The points to dwell upon are these: Every scholar in the four, with the exception of the marching flank, or the outside pupil, turns the face toward the marching flank, and dresses to the pivot, which, by the way, is not a fixed one. One reason why a company has trouble in rounding corners is that the pivots either fix themselves or take steps that are much too short, and the radius of the circle is not equal to half of the company front. This is an important rule, and should be strictly enforced. The wheeling on a fixed pivot with a small company front is not difficult, hence let all wheeling be begun with squads. Increase the size of these until the entire class can wheel to the right or the left. But the rule must be observed that the eyes are upon the marching flank and the elbows touch to the pivots. The marching flank pupil takes the regulation step, and from this point down to the pivot the step is gradually shortened. Another important bit of advice to be remembered is: In case those in the center do not shorten the step, the line will bulge to the front. Wheeling requires practice and patience on the part of both instructor and pupils. Wheeling on a movable pivot is much harder than when the stationary form is used. By following the directions given in the text, this work can be well done.

To form a column of fours from a column of twos or files. (Fig. 18.) Marching in column of twos the teacher commands, "Form fours, left (or right) oblique, *march!*" At the command *march*, the leading two of each four take the short step; the rear two oblique to the left until they uncover the leading two, when they resume the forward march. Having formed column of files from column of twos or fours, to form column of fours the teacher commands, "Form fours, left (or right) oblique, *march!*" At the command *march*, number one of the first four moves forward three yards and halts; the other files of the first four oblique to the left and place themselves successively on the left of the leading file; the other fours successively form as explained for the first.

Column of twos is formed from column of files on the same principles. (Fig. 19.)

In forming column of fours, or twos, the teacher commands, "Left (or right) oblique," according as the right or left is in front.

It is understood that the scholars have counted fours. It may seem

FIG. 18.—Form Fours from Twos.

strange to some that attention is drawn to this seemingly plain point, but more than one teacher has started a class around the room and given the command to form twos and fours, when the pupils had not been numbered.

To form twos from a column of files is different from forming twos from a line. These terms are confusing, and the new teacher is frequently bothered by the similarity between them. It is enough for one lesson to teach forming twos and fours from a file; but our ambitious teacher attempts to teach at one lesson much of what is found in the chapter on military training.

Children are taught by the picture method. It is one of the easiest ways to educate a person. So in teaching the members of a class to form twos from a line of files, it is well to take the two leading files off to one side, where they can be seen by the entire class, and illustrate the method with them.

The salient features are these: The pupils must understand in which direction they are to go when they form twos on the right. Have the class count *twos* and then face to the right, so that they are in single file, then asking number one to stand perfectly still, request number two to step out to his right when the command is given. Then when the next order is given, viz.: "Left by file, *march!*" have number two step back to the file. Try the same plan when the class is in motion, but insist upon number one

FIG. 19.—Form Twos from a File.

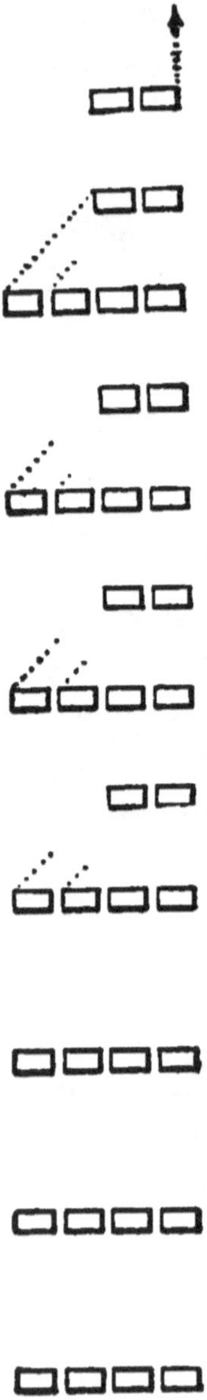

shortening the step, number two obliquing to the right and lengthening the step, and explain to the class that this is necessary to keep the distance. I should illustrate forming fours from twos or from a file by the same picture method. In forming a column of fours from a file, it is just as well to have number one mark time as soon as the command *march* is given, rather than to take three steps forward, as given in the old tactics. To form twos from a column of fours, command, "Right (or left) by twos, *march!*" (See Fig. 20.)

To form column of twos from line, the teacher commands, "Twos, right (or left), *march!*" The twos wheel to the right on numbers one and three of each four as pivots, and to the left on numbers two and four. The column of twos is formed in line by the commands, "Twos, left (or right), *march!* Guide right (or left)"; "Company, halt! Right (or left) dress, *front!*" The line is formed to the *left* or *right*, according as the right or left is in front.

To form twos from a line is different from forming twos from a file. The commands are not the same. I would impress it upon the mind of the young

Fig. 20.—Form Twos from Fours.

MILITARY GYMNASTICS. 211

teacher that the first word in the command when forming twos from files must be remembered, viz.: the word *form*. To form twos from a line, the command is, "Twos, right (or left), *march!*" The movement is easily learned, and not a difficult one to teach. Remember this: that as soon as the twos are formed from the line they march ahead, and do not stop unless they have the command to do so. If we wish to form a line from a column of twos, the command will be given, "Twos, right (or left), *march!*" in which case the pivot is on the left or the right, according to the command. It is not necessary to take time to explain these, only the scholars must remember that after the movement has been executed they march directly ahead, if no other command is given, and dress, according to the rules for marching in a line. If the teacher wishes to form fours from a line, the command will be, "Fours, right (or left), *march!*" after which number one (or four) is to act as a fixed pivot, and four (or one) the marching flank. The rules for wheeling must be observed, even when applied to a three or a four. While speaking of a four, let me call attention to the commands, "Fours, right about (or left about), *march!*" in which case the marching flank goes over 180 degrees. The pivot is fixed; the rules for wheeling are to be observed. If the instructor wishes the four to march completely around in a circle, the command is, "Fours in circle, right (or left) wheel, *march!*" in which case the pivot is a fixed one, and the rules for wheeling are observed. The four continues to march around in a circle until the command *halt*, or "Forward, *march!*" or "Mark time, *mark!*" is given.

To march in column of fours to the front. Being in line the teacher commands, "Right (or left), *forward*, fours right (or left), *march.*" (Fig. 21.) At the command *march*, the right four moves straight to the front, shortening the first three or four steps; the other fours wheel to the right on a fixed pivot; the second four, when its wheel is two thirds completed, wheels to the

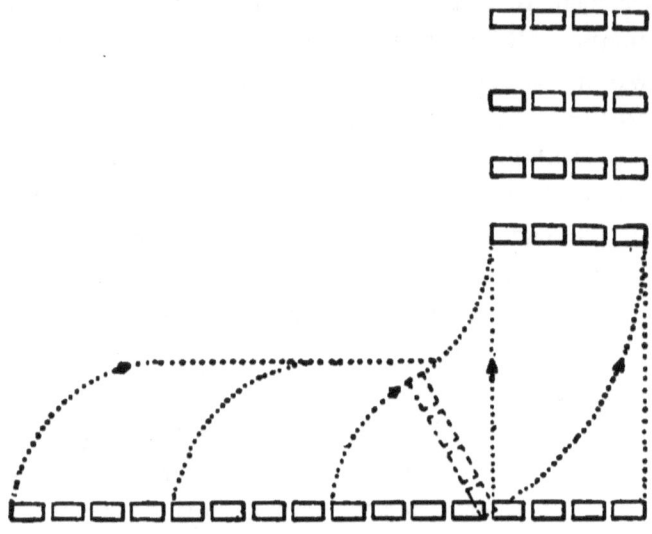

FIG. 21.—Right, Forward, Fours Right.

left on a movable pivot, and follows the first four; the other fours, having wheeled to the right, move forward and wheel to the left on a movable pivot on the same ground as the second.

To march in a column of fours to the front, the scholars are in a line; the command is found in the description. At the command *march*, the first four must shorten the first few steps. Teachers do not emphasize this, consequently there is an irregular space between the first and the second four. The second four in the line has the hardest work to do, because part of its work is on a fixed and part on a movable pivot. It is well, therefore, for the teacher to explain carefully to the second four just what they are to do. The result will be that, when the column of fours is formed and marched to the front, the lines are regular and the spaces even. The rules for turning a corner in a column of fours have been given. Dwell upon the fact that the pivots are movable, that the elbows touch the pivot, and the eyes are turned toward the marching flank until the wheel is made, when the eyes are again turned to the front.

There is one command that is somewhat irregular, but nevertheless the movement is of so much value that I use it frequently. It is to form fours or threes or sixes by a flank movement. The command is, "First four by the right flank, *march!*" At the command *march*, the first four face to the right and march in the new direction, *shortening the steps*. The rest of the file will march to the same point, and each four will, in turn, execute the right flank movement and march in the new direction. By this plan the scholars can take their numbers and form their fours in one movement. The teacher must emphasize the fact that each number one must wait for two, three, and four before marching in the new direction, as otherwise the four form an irregular line.

In closing the chapter upon military drill, I wish to state that too much importance cannot be attached to this part of our physical training. The scholar who has been well drilled in this respect acquires control over the body. It is said that we can pick out a West Pointer at a glance. It is true that we associate with the officer in the army the erect carriage, the firm step, and the proud bearing, which military drill will give. The men who compose the army are, to a certain extent, machines. Their work becomes automatic, and they obey commands without thinking. They are to use their best energies in fighting. While this, of course, does not apply to the scholars in our schools, nevertheless that boy or girl who has received some military training will exhibit its good effects in other ways. It is true that the head is erect, the chest in a better position, the movements of the body are decided and regular, and the child is more apt to show the results of the discipline in better mental work than one who has not been so trained.

I am aware that in many of our schools the military training is a farce. The fault is not entirely that of the teacher, but of the principal of the school, who does not wish, or who is not in a position to enforce, strict obedience. In this part of our training the body is always ready for immediate action. No time is lost. The pupil does not stand with the weight back upon the heels, but is well poised, and starts forward upon the command, or steps in any one of the given directions.

I have taken some time to speak of what may seem to be too simple details, but my experience with a large number of teachers has shown me that they do not understand the rudiments of this work, and I would strongly urge that the man or woman who teaches military drill try the movements and practice them before attempting to teach them to a class of boys or girls.

At what age should we teach military drill in our schools? As soon as we begin to teach gymnastics.

CHAPTER XVII.

USE OF LIGHT APPARATUS.

DUMB BELLS.

IT is perhaps not necessary to dwell at length upon the comparative value of the dumb bells, Indian clubs, and wands. The three pieces of apparatus should be used. There is, perhaps, a greater variety of movement to be found with the wands and the bells than with the clubs, when we take into consideration the movements of the body combined with those of the arms. The wands and Indian clubs will be discussed under special headings.

Regarding the bells, experience teaches us that two weights are sufficient, viz.: the one-pound wooden dumb bell, for pupils over ten years of age—this to include the young men in the gymnasium; for pupils under ten the half-pound bell will answer. The best bell to use is one with a large handle. The old style fancy dumb bell, with slender, curved handles, is not strong enough for gymnasium use. Bells should be made of hard wood, with an oil finish. The teacher should insist upon securing those which are not shellaced. With proper use, they ought to last a number of years.

The various manufacturers have placed on the market racks of different kinds for holding the bells. These racks should be placed in different parts of the room. Do not have the bells placed together in a certain portion of the gymnasium, because, if the scholars are allowed to break ranks to secure them, there will be rushing and crowding. It is better to scatter them on three or four sides of the room, and to place between the pairs of bells a pair of Indian clubs.

The question has been asked, How soon can we begin to use the dumb bells in the gymnasium? They can be given to the members of the smaller class, although it is better to give the children and pupils in the kindergarten department exercises included under the term free gymnastics. Certainly it is not advisable to give them the bells until after Christmas, if the school opens in September. This is also true of the wands. We do not give the Indian clubs to the children until they have been in the gymnasium for one, two, or more years.

The bells may be taken from the racks in several ways. The plan adopted by some teachers is to have the class march around the room, each pupil taking from the racks a pair of bells as he marches by. This is a good way if the class has been drilled in military work.

A short lesson upon this subject may assist the teacher. Let us imagine that the class is to take the bells for the first time. The teacher will call attention to this piece of apparatus; will perhaps take her own bells from the rack connected with the platform and show them to the children. She should then make the statements, which form part of the discipline of the class, *i. e.*, that the pupils will be allowed to take the apparatus if they show by their actions that they are old enough. They must under no conditions strike the bells together until they have permission to do so, while the scholar who drops his bell on the floor shows that he is not strong enough or is not well enough drilled to hold it in his hands.

The great difficulty will be the "clicking" of the bells, which almost immediately follows the first trial. It is the fault of the teacher if it happens. The instructor should anticipate these difficulties, warn the class, and enforce her orders.

It now remains to be seen whether the teacher has the courage of her convictions, and will keep her word with the class. She will give the pupils in the first row permission to step across to the racks, take their bells, and return to places. When they have come back to position the bells should be placed on the hips. The scholars will then be compelled to remain standing still for a very short time, while the pupils in the other rows get their supply and come back to position. Very likely it will happen that, while the scholars in the third or fourth row are getting their bells, some one in the first row will disobey the order and strike the bells together, either in front or back of the body. The teacher must at once ascertain the offender, and request him to replace immediately his bells in the rack. The effect upon the rest of the class will be a good one. They know then that the teacher means what she says. It is doubtful if there need be a repetition of this punishment in the class, if the teacher acts without delay in the case of the first offense.

After all members of the class have supplied themselves with bells, it may be well for the teacher to allow the scholars to examine them, and to strike them together if necessary. It is true that this clicking will make a loud noise, but no harm will result. The curiosity of the child will have been satisfied, and he is less likely to violate rules in the future. I have very often tried this plan, and found that it works well.

If the first wish of the children is to make a noise with the bells, give them a lesson in which they can make all the noise they wish, such as striking the bells in front of the body or above the head, in unison. At the close of the lesson the teacher should see that the bells are put back in *the same places from which they were taken.* If there are two sizes used in the class, the necessity for this will be evident. Otherwise the large bells will be mixed up with the smaller ones, and *vice versâ.* As soon as the teacher has impressed it thoroughly upon the class that they are not to rap their dumb bells, and that dropping them is out of the question, she can proceed to the next step, which is to drill the class in taking the bells, coming back to position, letting the arms hang at the side and not twisting the arms. I should strongly urge a teacher to be careful about making rules that she is not in a position to enforce. It is not wrong for a child to twist the arm when the bell is held in the hand, nevertheless, as a part of its training, he should be taught to hold the arms at the side. It would be poor teaching to request a class of children to hold the bells for a long time without taking some exercise. In such a case the scholars may be excused if they violate rules. It is the idle class that gets into trouble. Keep the class busy during the entire period allotted for the lesson in gymnastics.

Another difficulty that the teacher will have to meet is the changing of the bells. A scholar secures one pair and goes to his place; they do not suit him and he starts back to make a change. Do not allow this. Then there is, in the class, a very particular scholar, who will try to find two bells of exactly the same color and shape. He will pick out one bell, and start to run up and down the room to find another that is exactly like it. This, of course, must not be tolerated.

What shall we give at the first lesson? If the children have been well drilled in taking, holding, and replacing the bells, much has been accomplished, and this is enough for the first lesson. For the interesting part of the drill the scholars may be permitted to go through some of the striking motions mentioned above. The running in place can be given at the same time, allowing them to strike the bells, first the thumb ends and then the little finger ends, the bells being held chest high to the front, the arms bent. The simplest motions must be given at the beginning. As we teach the alphabet, or the sounds of the letters, to the child beginning to read, so we should give the simple attitudes, positions, or exercises with the dumb bells.

The movements should be given in the simplest time. To illustrate: One teacher, in giving a class of children a drill with the dumb bells, requested them to take the alternate movements. As the children had never heard the word "alternate" before, they did not know what she meant, and although she showed the exercise, they did not do the movements at all well. It is better to give movements with one arm, or possibly with two; but do not make the exercise complex or compound at the start. The thrusting and swinging movements with the arms are easily taught and learned. The circling motion with the arm is harder. (The reader is referred to "Light Gymnastics" for the alphabet with the dumb bells.)

Imitation work is always good for children and adults. By this it is meant that the teacher is to take an exercise without describing it, slowly at first, but afterwards the movements can be given rapidly. This always arouses a great deal of interest and merriment on the part of the children. The child sees the picture, and is compelled to imitate it as quickly as possible. This, of course, will require attention, observation, and muscular or nerve control on the part of the little ones.

Professor Morrill, of the State Normal School at New Haven, says that he believes the muscle sense in a child can be developed, and that it is educated quicker if the child is allowed to take the movement in order that he may *feel* the exercise. The person who draws himself up and turns over on the horizontal bar experiences a certain feeling that he will always associate with that particular exercise. On the other hand, the one who cannot do this will never have experienced that peculiar sensation which Professor Morrill calls the "muscle sense." So with a child: the one who has taken a certain exercise accurately will experience the sensation which follows a movement well executed, and this will assist him in the future in doing accurate work.

The picture method of teaching an exercise has been mentioned elsewhere in this book. It is valuable, but should not be overdone. The teacher should explain an exercise without showing it, and request the scholars to take it. This will require thought and will power on the part of the child. It would not be wise to give work of this character to a class of children who had been taking an examination or were wearied with mental effort.

When pupils have been drilled in marching and can keep step, and the work is to a certain extent automatic, the teacher might frequently allow them to march for the dumb bells and come back to places. It will require, however, an alert disciplinarian to keep order if this is done. Pupils will often strike the bells against the sides of the room or against the bells of their neighbor, and do it on the side not seen by the teacher; but this can be stopped at once if, as has been said, the teacher is alert and wide awake. The first offense must be treated without delay.

When a drill is taken, if the work has not been well done, repeat it. This applies to any exercise. Do not let a class think that you are satisfied with a movement that is but half done. When marching for the bells or taking any position, so far as it is possible, the teacher should insist upon accurate work, and while individual effort cannot be noticed so well, the glaring mistakes can be corrected while the drill is progressing.

The combinations with the dumb bells are many. The various drills and exercises are numerous, attractive, and valuable. Apart from these special drills, it is well frequently to give the class specific work for the arms (see "Hints on Teaching Boys"), making that the subject of the lesson; on another day, special work for widening and deepening the chest. That is the lesson which is to be remembered. The scholar should be taught something new every day, and if a series of movements is given that will develop the muscles on the front and back of the forearm, it should be so taught that it is impressed upon his mind. Do not expect that everything given will be remembered.

Such exercises as the Anvil Chorus, or the Pizzicati, or the Dumb Bell Quadrille have been criticised, on the ground that they are showy and pretty. It is true that they are of the æsthetic kind, but they require muscular effort, self-control, and grace of movement, and requiring these, they produce them.

Some of our teachers make a mistake in allowing too long an interval between exercises of the same kind. For example, an instructor will begin the Anvil Chorus, teach the first third one week, and not take up the second part until two weeks later. It may extend over from one to two months, so that the child loses some of his interest in this special drill. The exercise mentioned is only a sample. Do not be in a hurry when teaching gymnastics. If, perchance, the teacher is acquainted with the drill which is now somewhat *passe*, the Anvil Chorus, I would suggest that she divide this combination of exercises into three parts, the first of which includes the quiet exercises, arm and leg movements, the second, the striking movements with the bells, while the third comprises one or two striking and a number of silent movements, also the finish of the drill. There is in the first part something noticeable that will make this portion of the drill easily remembered, *i. e.*, that every movement is repeated, and all are taken on both the right and the left sides. The teacher who will analyze the arrangement of a drill will find that there are many little things that she can remember that will be of great assistance in teaching the exercise. Often, when giving instruction of this character, the teacher will, for the time being, forget what is coming next. This forgetfulness produces temporary embarrassment, which will be noticed by the scholars and the accompanist and will affect the teaching. One who is placed in this position can go back and repeat some exercise or some portion of the drill, in order to gain time to collect her scattered thoughts.

A good combination of movements with the dumb bells is marking time in place, combined with simple arm flexions, extensions, arm swingings, or with striking motions. They are, however, rather harder to teach than the marching movements taken with the same exercises. At first all such combinations should be simple. Do not teach too many at one lesson ; rather give the pupils a drill in the few than the many. When marching around the room, if both sexes are represented in the class, we have frequently had the girls march in one direction and take the outside track, and the boys march in another direction, taking the inside track. The reason for this is that the girls, as a rule, behave better than the boys. If the latter were allowed to take the outside course and were given the thrusting movements with the bells, they would take great delight in striking the walls or the apparatus. It is well to avoid thrusting the arms out when marching. They can be thrust up or down without requiring too much space. The circling motions can be given to slow march time.

In Watson's "Calisthenics" will be found a number of very good double drills, but they should not be given unless the discipline is the very best. Whenever two scholars come together they try to have a good time.

There are a number of games that can be used with the bells, that we used to give to our classes on Friday, such as passing the dumb bells, which is something like passing bean bags, telegraphing with the bells, or the relay race. Telegraphing is done in this fashion: The scholars stand side by side, almost at arm's length, facing the center of the room, with a dumb bell in each hand. The teacher stands at the head of the line and strikes the bell of the first pupil, who in turn strikes the bell of the second pupil, and thus the sound is carried down the class, each striking the bell upon the right or the left, the last in the line dropping his bell upon the floor as soon as the "telegram" reaches him. The game is rather an exciting one, and interesting. The relay race is this: Ten boys are matched against ten girls. The first boy walks around the room as rapidly as he can, carrying a dumb bell. In order that he may not cut the corners, a boy is stationed at each around whom he will have to walk. When he reaches the starting point he stops walking, passes the bell to the second one in the class, who, in turn, walks around and hands it to the third. Thus, in a very short time the ten boys have walked around the room. The time has been recorded by the teacher, who will in the same way test the girls.*

THE WANDS.

There are many rules common to the wands, bells, and clubs. It is not necessary to repeat them if they have been given under any one of the special headings. The physical director who uses these light appliances should read the articles as they are given in this book. In discipline, for example, the rule against dropping a bell applies to the wand. The teacher must be careful that the pupils do not get the start in dropping wands. It makes a great deal of noise, and if one starts others will follow. It will be a source of pleasure to the class, and annoyance to the teacher.

Children should be allowed to use the wands as soon as they are old enough to exercise with the bells. The variety of work is great. The wand, if it is made of a proper length and diameter, can be used as a gun, in which case the manual of arms and bayonet drill will be found valuable and interesting. The teacher, however, must avoid the error of supposing that the drill is the end of the exercise, and not the means to an end. The small dowels that can be purchased at many of the hardware stores can be used as well as the more expensive wand. The author has purchased these at the rate of one cent each. They can be sandpapered, and will serve very well for the other uses to which the wand can be put, viz.: the broadsword drill for public schools, the single stick, and double and compound work.

Arrange the wands in somewhat the manner recom-

---

* For other games see Anderson's "Chautauqua Primer of Gymnastics."

mended for the dumb bells, but place them in boxes in different parts of the room. Racks are found in some of the gymnasia, but are not so good as the boxes, on account of the time required to take and replace wands.

How to take the wands is a matter worth considering. The teacher should explain the method of holding the stick. Many will grasp the wand incorrectly, as seen in the illustration. (Fig. 22.) To make this plainer to the children, tell them to hold the wand as they would hold a pen, or as in Fig. 23, in which case it rests in the notch made by the thumb and first finger. This, of course, is a small point, but only attention to detail will bring good results. The question has come up a number of times whether a child should hold the wand at carry arms, or down. (Fig. 24.) For many reasons, the former method is preferable, although more difficult to teach.

The teacher should give wands to the scholars after they have been well grounded in the fundamental principles of free gymnastics. She should warn them about disobeying the few rules that are made, and call their attention to dropping the wand or moving it away from the body. If the scholars are anxious to take the wands the teacher should take advantage of their desire, but the business part of the drill comes when the few rules are made. It is better for the teacher to appoint monitors, the first or last in each row, or any special scholar in whom she has confidence, to step to one box, select a sufficient number of wands for those in the file, then take a standing position at the head of the row. When all the monitors are so placed, the teacher gives the command for the distribution, when the monitors step down and hand a wand to each pupil.

We must make some allowance for the boy or girl who means to do well, but occasionally forgets. A child, for example, unwittingly violates a rule, and is requested to return the wand to the box. It is not wise to be too severe in a case of this kind. If the boy admits that he has made a mistake and is willing to do better in the future, allow him again to take the wand.

The objection to marching for the wands is the same as that to marching for bells. It should not be done until the class understands well the simple movements in military gymnastics. They are then to march in single file past the box, each pupil selecting a wand and bringing it to carry arms. They then proceed to their footmarks or positions on the floor.

The teacher should give the class a drill in taking and replacing the wands. Do not be too anxious to begin the exercise. If the chief part of the first lesson is given to the method of securing apparatus, the children will be apt to remember and more ready to obey the next time. If, on the other hand, the teacher is careless and is too anxious to proceed with the drill, here, as in other exercises, she must pay the penalty later on, and the blame for confusion, disorder, and poor work rests on her, and not on the scholars.

The simple alphabet of movements with the wand would include these terms: wand down, front, up, out to the right or left, right arm or left arm front or up, the right and left hand salutes, wand on the chest, wand front and twisted. These, of course, can be taken with

Fig. 22.—Carrying Wand Incorrectly. (Page 227.)

Fig. 23.—Method of Grasping Wand. (Page 227.)

Fig. 24.—Wand Down. (Page 227.)

Fig. 25.—The Single Pendulum. (Page 235.)

the stepping, foot placing, charging, and lunging motions. The combination of movements is almost countless. In addition to the simple and compound movements, the teacher can give the class instruction in the manual of arms, under which heading would come present, port, charge, order, firing, the kneeling movements, reverse arms, etc. (See "Light Gymnastics.") Special drills can be given for the development of different parts of the body, viz.: the arms, shoulders, front, back, and sides of the waist. Running exercises have been given, but the wand interferes with the action of the arms.

Too much value should not be placed upon the series with the wands. It is better that the drill should be given with some purpose in view, rather than an aimless line of exercises that are only for exhibition. The teacher at each lesson should give motions that will tend to draw the shoulders back to place, to widen and deepen the chest, to develop the muscles of the waist and back. Simple attitudes have been given, and are valuable because they require bodily control. The line work is good at times, but should not be given unless the scholars are well disciplined. As with the poles, pupils have an opportunity to play, and it is not easy to pick out the culprit. There are so many good drills that it is not necessary to take the space here for a description of any of them.

INDIAN CLUBS.

The work with the Indian clubs is always interesting. It is popular and there is a universal call for it. It is not easy for one to learn all that can be given in club swinging. While the simple movements that are taught at the first lessons may be mastered in a few weeks, the more difficult combinations, including the snakes and reverse snakes, will require long-continued practice. The value of club swinging has frequently been questioned, and there is no doubt that some of the movements tend to cramp the chest and to flatten its walls. On the other hand, the long circles to the right and left elevate the shoulders, produce vacuums in the apices of the lungs, so that for some forms of threatened lung trouble they are really beneficial. Another argument against club swinging is that only the arms and the trunk of the body are used. There would be some weight to this statement if it were true, but many of the exercises that are given require arm work combined with leg action. Dr. Seaver gave a club drill for a number of years which was about the same to Yale that the Hitchcock dumb bell drill was to Amherst. He succeeded in deriving as much benefit from the club movements as many teachers would from free gymnastics and with the bells. The arm swinging movements were combined with charging, lunging, and swaying exercises. In the German gymnastics one will see a combination of the long circles with stepping, facing, and turning movements. It is not wise for the teacher to confine her drills to circling motions, which too often necessitate standing still.

Frequently children are allowed to take but one club, in which case they hold it down, as they would a wand, when they are given the flexing movements of the arms, swinging the club front and up, combining these movements with stepping, charging, and swaying exercises.

The clubs should not be given to the children until they have been well grounded in the principles of free gymnastics and have used the wands and the bells. There is more danger when a class is beginning club swinging than when using any other piece of apparatus. The careless child will swing the club around the head and may strike the one standing upon the right or the left or immediately back of him. If the club slips and strikes some one the result may be serious. Again, the movements not well taught will result in injury to the person's own body. The lower front circle has been given in such a way that the child would strike his own face with the end of the club. Do not give two clubs to pupils at the first lesson.

A drill should be given in the method of taking and replacing clubs. The first time they are used the pupils in one line are allowed to break ranks, step to the racks, each scholar take one club, and come back to position. A stated time is allowed for the selection of apparatus, and if all the scholars are not back within this limit, then is the time for questioning. The children, after taking the apparatus, should stand strictly in place, the club in the right hand and at the side. Scholars who disobey should be punished immediately. A great penalty is replacing the club in the rack and doing only the arm work. At the close of the lesson the pupils, one row at a time, replace the clubs and return to footmarks. The teacher must look out for these difficulties: dropping the clubs, or letting them slip from the hand while making the circles. The children under no conditions should be allowed to make the circles while the other members of the class are taking or replacing their clubs.

A few words about the weight. Clubs should not weigh more than two pounds for the oldest and strongest classes. At Yale University the two-pound clubs are popular, the men preferring them to the "three-pounders." For children, three-quarter and half-pound clubs are suitable. There are numerous models made, but the one shown in the illustrations is recommended, on account of its shape, size, and what is called "the balance."

If a teacher thinks it is better to have the scholars march from files and take the clubs, and the classes are mixed, the girls should march first. They will obey rules better than boys, and do not swing their clubs back and forth when they have returned to their footmarks.

Frequently it happens that after a class has been placed upon the floor and is at work with clubs, scholars will enter the room and start at once for the footmarks. This is dangerous. The class should be brought to an immediate halt, or the scholar should be requested to come to the platform. The latter is preferable. The class should be drilled in halting instantly. It may be that one member of a class will drop the club, and if it goes rolling along the floor, he will, regardless of the danger, run after it, and very likely be struck by another pupil. If a club is dropped, the command *halt* should be given at once, and if the scholars are well drilled they will obey the command. It is better, however, to teach prevention than to cure, and the individual should be cautioned against attempting to secure the club. In some cases the hand will become moist from perspiration, and the club will easily slip. Again, if the fingers are fatigued, the club may drop. The scholar who is tired should not continue the exercise. Permission should be given him to stand at place rest with the club at the side.

In club swinging every movement and position should be analyzed. Only two directions are used in making the long circles, namely, to the right and the left, and front and rear. We do not, as a rule, swing the clubs in the oblique directions when making the complete or the long circles. It is well for the teacher at the start to indicate by a movement of the hand or head in which direction the club is to go.

In answer to the question, "How far apart should scholars stand when swinging two clubs?" they can stand six feet and take all double and follow work to the sides or to the front and rear, but reel work, where both arms swing out in different directions, should not be given. When pupils stand seven or more feet apart all circles can be taken.

There are only two kinds of circles in club swinging: first, the long one, in which the shoulder is near the center of the circle; second, the short one, or a wrist circle. The short circles are made at the shoulder, above the head, at arm's length in any direction, hip high in front, and back of the body—the latter being considered the hardest circles. A combination of any two circles is called a complete circle. For example, the child makes what is termed a heart-shaped circle to the right; he then makes the short circle at the shoulder. Making these two without a stop is a complete exercise. In the same way the complete lower front, the complete lower back, and the complete overhead circles are made.

A motion is made with two clubs to the right or left. This is called a *double* exercise. The circles are made to the right or the left with one club leading and the other club following. This is termed a *follow* circle. One club goes to the right and makes a long circle, while the other makes a short circle to the left. This would be called *reel time.*

The teacher is cautioned about using different terms for the same exercise. In our American system of gymnastics we have no nomenclature. One teacher may use her own terms; another teacher will use entirely different words for the same command. The instructor who will analyze every exercise will find that she can teach it better. The heart-shaped circle, for example, should be carefully dissected. It consists in starting the club from the fundamental position, raising the hand a little higher than the head, swinging out to the right, making almost a complete circle, and bringing it back to position. The pupil who wears tight clothing will make what is called a forearm circle, the elbow being near the center, rather than the shoulder.

The *pass* is a term frequently used. It means that the club is passed from the right to the left hand. It is used only when the pupils are exercising with one club.

If too much time has been given to the short or the complete shoulder circles, the shoulder should be rested, and the pendulum movements given. If it happens that the child is fatigued, stop the arm work for the time, and give the class a drill for the legs, such as the stepping or swaying motions, raising on the toes, or flexing the legs. A great mistake made by teachers is giving too much at one lesson.

Analysis of the drop circle. This consists of two movements—the double shoulder circles, and the double pendulum. Do not teach this until the class has been thoroughly drilled in each part. The single pendulum consists in swinging the club from right to left, shoulder high, as seen in the illustration. (Fig. 25.) Beginners will swing the clubs above the head. Unless the instructor emphasizes the necessity of stopping the clubs at the height of the shoulder she will not obtain good results. If, on the other hand, she will take a few seconds to say that the scholars should stop the clubs at a certain height and then permit them to swing the clubs to that position and stop them, she will add emphasis to her teaching.

Analysis of the reel. This consists of the complete shoulder circles out, the right hand going to the right and the left hand to the left. A method of teaching the exercise is this: Permit the scholars to make the heart-shaped circle with the left hand, the shoulder circle with the right hand, *out*. Let them take it a sufficient number of times to make it almost automatic. Next reverse this, and let them make the short circle with the left hand and the long circle with the right, and so continue until the circles are easily made with either arm. At the finish there is a short pause. Two counts are given for the motion. Later on they can pass to the "reel," which is a continuous movement.

236   METHODS OF TEACHING GYMNASTICS.

Analysis of the "snake." First teach pupils how to grasp the club. (Fig. 26.) The snake is made from a swinging start, either at the end of a short or long circle. The lower start is preferable, *i. e.*, with the club hanging at the side, in which case the arm is carried across the body and held as seen in the illustration. (Fig. 27.) From this position it is thrown around to the right and rests upon the top of the arm. The points to consider are these: the club is parallel to the floor; it is grasped by the second, third, and little fingers; the thumb is underneath, and the first finger upon the knob of the club. There are three parts to this movement, only one of which is to be taught at a lesson, viz.: the fundamental starting position, and the first circle, which is described thus:

The free end of the club is carried around under the chin, an important point to remember, because it insures a right start. At the end of the first third of the circle the club is held in this awkward position, the elbow well raised, the club in front of the chest and parallel to the floor. It continues around until the first circle is finished, at which time the club is under the arm, and is held as seen in Fig. 28.

The second is the hardest of the three. It is made by turning the back of the hand *in*, so that we have the position shown in Fig. 28. The free end of the club passes under the axilla, around in front of the chest, the hand going back, almost touching the side of the body, until the club, still parallel to the floor, rests on top of the forearm, the thumb being up, and the back of the hand to the front. This finishes the second circle. (See Fig. 29.)

FIG. 26.—The Grasp. (Page 236.)

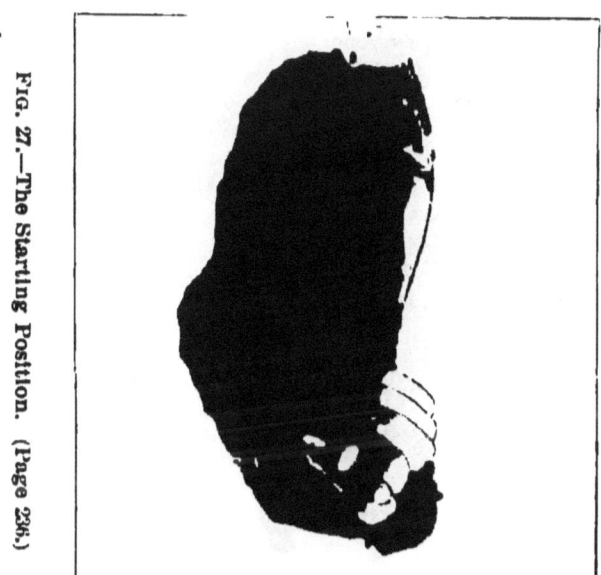

FIG. 27.—The Starting Position. (Page 236.)

Fig. 29.—Finish of the Second Circle. (Page 236.)

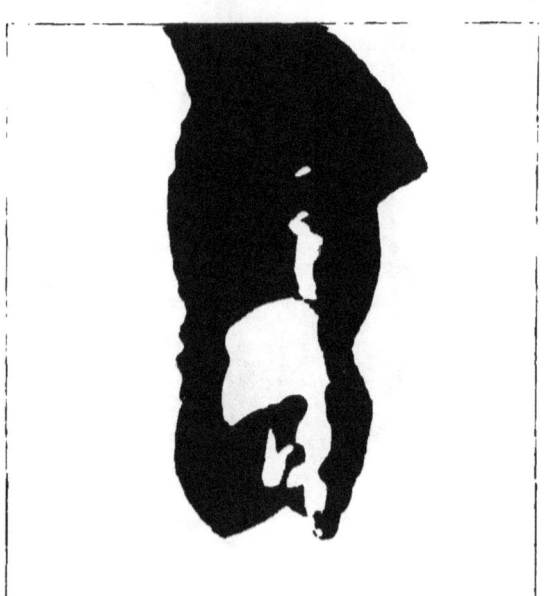

Fig. 28.—Start for the Second Circle. (Page 236.)

The third consists of a quick swing or (for lack of a better word) "sling," the club being thrown out and around and caught on the fleshy part of the arm in the starting position. (Fig. 27.) These three circles constitute the horizontal snake. If the motion is taken rapidly it can be made so that the hand does not go back, even with the side of the body.

Now take the swing out from the end of the second circle, to some other short or long circle. The second turn is finished with the club as seen in Fig. 29. To swing out for the lower front the hand is raised over the shoulders, the club pendant, from which position the club is again swung up, or we fling it up, which leaves us in position to make a lower back or lower front. Only two of the three snake circles are made, then the club is thrown out for some combination at the end of the second. The hard parts are the catch as the club is thrown into position and the first and second circles.

The difference between a horizontal and a perpendicular snake is that in the first the club is parallel to the floor, and in the second it is in a perpendicular position; of the two, the perpendicular snake is the harder.

There is what is called the half snake—a perpendicular movement. The club may swing from below or from the fundamental starting position out, make a long circle, and swing into the second of the movements which make the snake, the arm being shaped a little like a swan's neck (Fig. 30), from which position the circle is finished.

The reverse snake may be learned by making one

regular snake and then going back over the same ground. Better still, one part must be made at a time, and then the movement reversed.*

FENCING.

This exercise is reserved for advanced pupils. The drill that is set aside for scholars is called the school form of broadsword exercises. It is neither wise nor safe to allow the pupils in classes where masks are not worn to practice what may be termed the French or Italian system of foil fencing, in which the child thrusts or pokes his sword at another. In broadsword, all of the work consists of giving light blows, which may be easily and safely warded.

The implements used are wands or dowels. They are three feet in length and three quarters of an inch in diameter. They will break easily, but it does not cost much to replace them. The teacher will find that the young men take delight in striking hard blows, the result of which is the destruction of the dowel or fencing stick. If these strong young men are requested to pay for the swords they break, the loss will be reduced to a minimum.

A light wooden sword, with detachable handle, costing from fifteen to twenty-five cents, can be purchased from the firms which make a specialty of manufacturing gymnastic apparatus. This is more popular than the dowel, because it is furnished with handle and guard and it looks like a sword.

The swords may be kept in racks ; the dowels, which

---

* Address Dr. Luther Gulick, Springfield, Mass., for illustrated article on the snake.

serve the double purpose of swords and wands, should be kept in the boxes. If the scholars are old enough to take the fencing drill, they are sufficiently advanced to march for the swords.

The preliminary movements in fencing should be given before the scholar is allowed to take the sword. These include the positions of the feet, arms, and body, and the passing to what is called the position of "on guard." The method of teaching is this :

The pupils assume the fundamental standing position, which see. The command is given, "Scholars, left oblique (or half face to the left), *face!*" Next place the feet at right angles, in which case the right foot points directly to the front, the left foot to the left. It will require more time to place the feet properly than it does to turn the body 45°. Place the hands on the hips, where they are out of the way, and give the class a drill in bending the knees, as seen in the illustration. (Fig. 31.) This exercise should be repeated a number of times. Notice that the feet are on the floor, the heels are not raised, the eyes and face are to the front. After bending the knees, teach advancing the right foot two foot lengths straight to the front. The teacher must insist upon the scholar advancing the foot directly to the front, and not in an oblique direction. If after executing the half face to the left the foot rests upon one board or line running to the front, it should rest upon the same board or line when it is advanced two foot lengths to the front. The right arm may then be advanced directly to the front, then it can be bent until the elbow is about the height of the chest, the distance between the elbow and the chest being seven or eight inches. Scholars who tire easily will allow the elbow to rest against the side of the waist. This is wrong.

It will require one or two lessons to perfect the scholars in these preliminary light movements, but they should be thoroughly mastered before the sword is used.

After they are able to place the feet in a proper position and understand how the arms are held, permit them to take the sword, and in the seven counts which are described in "Light Gymnastics," page 178, pass to the position of "on guard." The difficult part to teach is the position of the sword, or right arm. The teacher should carefully analyze every position and every part of the attitude, before attempting to teach. She should also have rehearsed all before the mirror, working on her left side.

The striking movements are made in two ways: first, by swaying the body forward and extending the arm; second, by advancing the foot one foot length to the front, making what is called the three-quarter lunge. Scholars strike at their opponent's sword, instead of aiming at these parts of the body, the top of the head, the cheeks, the round of the shoulders, and the middle of the thighs. A mistake often made is this: Pupils do not advance the right foot far enough, or sway the body sufficiently, to touch their opponent. This is more apt to be the case when giving the leg blows. Still another mistake is the failure to return to the position of "on guard" after a blow has been struck. This should be corrected, otherwise scholars will always be careless about returning to the correct position, and it will be seen that either the arms are curved too much or the point of the sword is above the top of the head.

Fencing will tire out the right arm. It is well, therefore, to drill the scholars on the left side.

Many of the young ladies in our schools have been averse to taking the correct position with the feet. They prefer to stand with the knees perfectly straight. A little patience on the part of the teacher and this mistake will be remedied.

CHAPTER XVIII.

MANNERISMS.

One who has made a study of teachers, especially beginners, will have noticed the many useless motions made by her during a lesson—the swinging of the arms, the twitching of the fingers, the clutching at the dress, the changing of the position of the body. She gives a command, then takes a short step; gives another command, then steps backward; explains an exercise and steps to the right or the left—in short, moves from place to place, in an aimless way, every time she makes an explanation. Another teacher, while speaking to the class, will sway from one side to another; that one will arrange some portion of her dress; this one will bring the hand to the face or fix the collar. They too frequently clasp their hands in front of them, or rest the elbows on the hips if they are women, or clasp the hands back of them if they are men. The hands too often rest upon the hips. One man used to twirl his moustache when he gave new commands or was at all annoyed or embarrassed. Another would scratch his head every time he gave a certain command, or was in any way disturbed.

Teachers who make mistakes in speaking are apt to make some useless motion with some portion of the body. This is an evidence of embarrassment; it soon comes to be a habit. Sew up the pockets of some of our young men, and they would hardly know how to act in company. The average student puts his hands in his pockets on all occasions. It is a studied mannerism with many young men. In college there was a student who had the habit of looking at a certain place on the wall every time he recited. On one occasion he was removed to another part of the room and, when called upon to recite, failed in his lesson because he could not find this particular spot. Another had the habit of playing with his watch charm. One day this was quietly removed just before his recitation. The result was a signal failure when he was called upon to recite.

There are ministers, teachers, lawyers, who are addicted to certain useless movements. For example, one minister invariably unbuttoned his coat, placed his handkerchief on the Bible, wiped his face with the handkerchief, and arched his chest, before he began the long prayer. The author, as a boy, watched this man every Sunday, and wondered if his prayer was better because of the extra movements. Teachers stand in place rest while giving instruction to the class or leading in military drill. The plan is a bad one. Few instructors can stand well while teaching. Some mannerisms are amusing, others are disagreeable. It is, of course, not always desirable for a teacher to stand perfectly still while directing a class, but there are times when she should, and when the time comes she cannot. It is recommended that teachers practice controlling themselves while standing before their pupils. The members of the class will very often unconsciously imitate the St. Vitus-like motions of the teacher. In one case, where the instructor was very much stooped, the little children tried their best to stand as if they were suffering from kyphosis.

The nervous, irritable teacher seems to have harder work than the phlegmatic one, but the power to overcome mannerisms is, to some extent, an acquired one. There is hardly an argument in favor of these unnecessary motions. They indicate lack of self-control; they show nervousness, embarrassment, awkwardness, and are frequently unpleasant to the pupil and to the teacher. They are indications of wasted energy. The teacher who does not know what her mannerisms are should ask some candid friend to tell her when she makes mistakes. If she will watch other teachers, she will very soon see that the statements made under this heading are not exaggerated. Let the teacher make a study of herself, and she need not call on any of her friends to criticise her. It might be well for the one who reads this article to see whether there is a beam in her own eye before she attempts to remove the mote from her sister's. That these errors should be corrected there is no doubt. They detract much from the teacher's personal appearance. While physical education will be apt to cause mannerisms as quickly as any other profession, at the same time the teacher can, if she wishes, overcome the tendency quicker than those who do not pay attention to muscular training. Of course, will power is needed, and in return, will power is developed if the defect is remedied. The author calls to mind only two of his many instructors who could stand perfectly still while leading a class.

CHAPTER XIX.

DIVISION OF WORK FOR THE MONTH AND DAY.

MILITARY GYMNASTICS.

BELOW will be found an arrangement of lessons for a class of beginners. This can be given to a normal class in three months, after which time the teacher can give any of the work found in "Light Gymnastics," using her own judgment as to the kind and amount.

The teacher should make a certain part of the drill a "lesson"; that is, she should give something new, should see that the class learns it, and then she can give any review work.

The author generally adds a little to what is found in the list, but it is something the class has had before.

Lesson No. 1.

Fall in.
Align.
Dressing.
Position of a soldier, or Attention.
Place rest.
Break ranks.

Lesson No. 2.

Right, left, and oblique face.
Marking time by
Stamping, tapping.
Swing the leg.

METHODS OF TEACHING GYMNASTICS.

Regular method.
Halt from marking time.

Lesson No. 3.

About facing, German and American methods.

Lesson No. 4.

The start.
Marching in a file.
Turning corners.
Halting.

Lesson No. 5.

Changing direction.
Column right and left.
Column half right and left.
Counter marching to right and left.

Lesson No. 6.

Cadence. Common time.
Short step.
Back step.

Lesson No. 7.

Side step.
Quick time.

Lesson No. 8.

Double time.

Lesson No. 9.

March in a line.
Guides.

Lesson No. 10.

Oblique marching.

Lesson No. 11.

Form twos from a file.
Right and left by file.

DIVISION OF WORK.

Lesson No. 12.
Form fours from file.
Right by twos.
Right by file.

Lesson No. 13.
Change step.

Lesson No. 14.
To the rear, march.

Lesson No. 15.
Marching by the flank.

Lesson No. 16.
Marching four abreast and turning corners.
Marching four abreast and keeping distance.

Lesson No. 17.
Fours right or left.

Lesson No. 18.
Fours right or left about.

Lesson No. 19.
Fours in circle.

Lesson No. 20.
Opening files.

Lesson No. 21.
Wheeling on a fixed pivot.

Lesson No. 22.
Wheeling on a movable pivot.

Lesson No. 23.
Oblique marching two and four abreast.

Lesson No. 24.
From column of twos form a line.
From a line form column of twos.

Lesson No. 25.
From line form fours.
From fours form line.
Lesson No. 26.
Right, forward, fours right.
Lesson No. 27.
On the right or left into line.
Lesson No. 28.
In double ranks form company.

FREE GYMNASTICS.

Arrangement of lessons in light gymnastics for the gymnastic year for a normal class.

There is such a great variety of work to be given under this heading that it will be impossible to give anything like a complete list or to classify all the movements.

The teacher understands that these arrangements are tentative to a degree, that they will be modified with experience, and that they do not take the place of the regular drill in body building.

If the author should make any criticism it would be that too much is given at a single lesson.

Lesson No. 1.
Planes of body.
Directions.
Arms down, up, front, out.
Lesson No. 2.
A typical lesson. (Follow the day's order.)
Feet open and close.
Foot placing. Figs. 12 and 14.
Lesson No. 3.
Stepping exercise. Fig. 10.

DIVISION OF WORK.

Lesson No. 4.

Order movements.
Hips firm. Fig. 32.
Neck firm. Fig. 33.
Letter Y. Fig. 6.
Clasping hands.
Arms folded.

Lessons Nos. 5 and 6.

The charging motion. Fig. 11.

Lesson No. 7.

The reverse charge. Fig. 13.

Lesson No. 8.

The swaying motions.

Lesson No. 9.

Wide and narrow bases.

Lessons Nos. 10 and 11. Subject, the head.

Bending and turning.
Rolling.
Oblique movements.
Forcing.
Resistance.

Lesson No. 12. Subject, the leg.

Heel raising.
Foot flexing.
Foot extension and circling.
(This is for ankle, front, and back leg.)

Lesson No. 13. Subject, hip and thigh.

Flex leg.

Lesson No. 14.

Flex thigh.
Bend and straighten the knee.
Thigh swinging.

Lesson No. 15.
Lunging.
Stamping.

Lesson No. 16. Subject, swaying.
Swaying with common and wide base.

Lesson No. 17. Subject, running.
Hopping and running.

Lesson No. 18. Subject, the arm.
Opening and closing the hand.
Separate and close the fingers.
Flex and extend the hand.
Circling the hand.

Lesson No. 19.
Flex and rotate the arm.
Arm swinging.
Thrusting motions.

Lesson No. 20. Subject, the arm, walking.
Work for wrist by all forearm motions.
Walking, knee bending, thigh flexing, leg swinging.

Lesson No. 21.
The seven primary exercises in walking.

Lesson No. 22. Subject, gesture work.
Angle work with arms.
Curved lines for gesture.

Lesson No. 23. Subject, compound work.
Charging motions with arms swinging.

Lesson No. 24. Subject, gesture work.
Curved lines combined with swaying motions.
Attitudes, first group.

Lesson No. 25.
Attitudes one and two.

DIVISION OF WORK.

Lesson No. 26.

Methods of placing the class.

Lesson No. 27. Subject, balancing exercises.

Toe standing with
Arms front, up, out.
Same, feet close.
Review charging and walking exercises.

Lesson No. 28. Subject, balancing.

Stride toe standing with
Arms up, front, out.
Same walk toe standing.
Review placing the class.

Lesson No. 29. Subject, balancing.

Balance step.
Attitude No. 4.

Lesson No. 30. Subject, balancing.

Walk standing with half-bent knees.
Same stride stand.
Attitude No. 5.

Lesson No. 31. Subject, balancing.

Flex legs.
Flex thighs.
Same with arms up, front, out.
Review all attitudes.

Lesson No. 32. Subject, shoulders.

Round shoulders.
Primary: force, elevate,
  depress, roll.
Secondary: setting up exercises.
Circling motions.
Attitudes good and bad.

Lesson No. 33. Subject, shoulders, lunging.

Uneven shoulders.
Elevate or shrug.
Secondary : arm swinging.
Head bending.
Lunging exercise.

Lesson No. 34. Subject, shoulders, lunging.

Bottle neck.
Head bending to right and left.
Arm swinging out and up.
Shrugging shoulders.
Lunging exercises.

Lesson No. 35. Subject, the thorax.

To widen.
Primary : sternum expression.
Secondary : shrug shoulders.
Swing arm sideways.
Bend body to right and left.   Letter Y.

Lesson No. 36. Subject, the thorax.

To deepen.
Primary : sternum expression.
Secondary : bend head backward.
Bend body backward.
Swing arms front and up.
Letter Y and bend backward.
Hips firm and forward bend.

Lesson No. 37. Subject, the lungs.

Breathing by inhaling and exhaling in rhythm.
Secondary : inhale and exhale and
Bend head backward.
Swing arms front and up, out and up.
Percussing motions for the thorax.

Fig. 30.—Start for the Half Snake. (Page 237.)

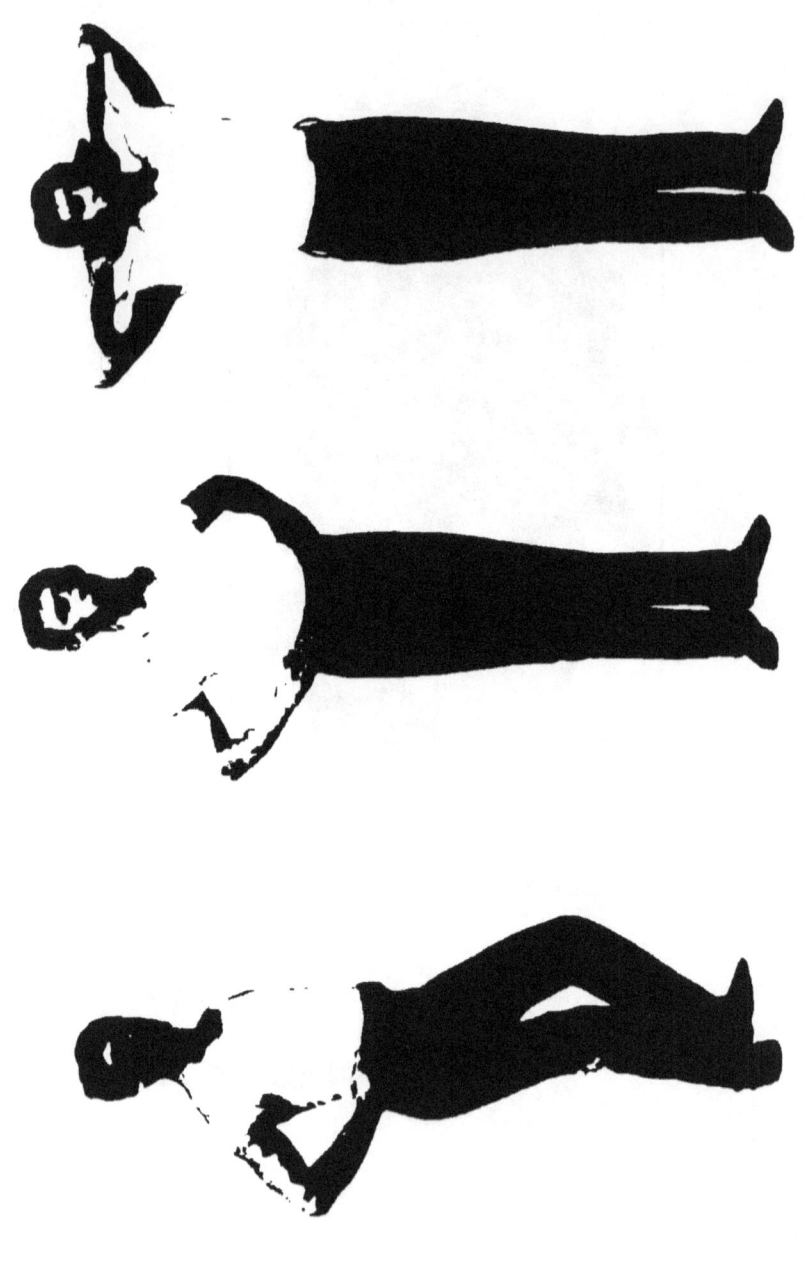

Fig. 31.—Knees Bent for Fencing. (Page 239.)   Fig. 32.—Hips Firm. (Page 249.)   Fig. 33.—Neck Firm. (Page 249.)

DIVISION OF WORK.

Lessons Nos. 38 and 39. Subject, the heart and lungs.
Preparation to jump.
Hopping exercises.
Running exercises.
Precipitant work.

Lesson No. 40. Quieting exercises.
Slow leg work.
Breathing.

Lesson No. 41. Subject, the hips.
Swing legs to front, right,
Back and obliquely back.
Bend body forward.

Lesson No. 42. Subject, the back.
Bend the body forward with
Hips firm, neck firm, and arms up.

Lesson No. 43. Subject, sides of the waist.
Bend the body to right and left with
Hips firm, neck firm, and arms up.

Lesson No. 44. Subject, the abdomen.
Bend body backward with
Hips firm, neck firm, and arms up.

Lessons Nos. 45, 46, and 47.
Postures.

Lessons Nos. 48, 49, and 50.
Percussing movements.

The following lessons have been used by the author in the public schools of the state of Connecticut:

Lesson No. 1.

Order Exercises: Position of attention, hips firm, arms down, out, up, and front.
Leg: Feet close, feet open; foot placing to right and left.
Head: Head backward bend; upward raise.

Arm: Flex and extend fingers, with arms down, front, and up.
Balancing: Stand on tiptoes, feet open.
Shoulder: Force shoulders back, touching scapula.
Thorax: Shrug shoulders.
Waist: Hips firm, body backward bend.
Back: Hips firm, body forward bend.
Heart and Lungs: Hopping on the right, then on the left foot.
Quieting: Foot placing to right and left.
Breathing: Shrug shoulders.

Lesson No. 2.

Order Exercises: Toe standing; neck firm; arms flexed.
Leg: Stepping motions.
Head: Neck firm, backward bend.
Arm: Flexing and extending of hand, with arm in four positions.
Balancing: Standing on toes, feet close.
Shoulders: Hips firm, thumbs touching back of body.
Thorax: Arms swinging front.
Waist: Hips firm, body backward bending.
Back: Forward bending. Hips firm, feet close.
Heart and Lungs: Hopping on right and left foot.
Quieting: Stepping motions.
Breathing: Arm swinging front.

Lesson No. 3.

Order Exercises: Upton's position of a soldier. Walk stand, hips firm, arms one-half flexed.
Leg: Calf work, raise on toes.
Head: Head to right and left bend.
Arms: Rotate forearms, arms half flexed.
Balancing: Walk toe standing.
Shoulders: Flex arms, palms front.
Thorax: Arm swinging out.
Waist: Hips firm, body bending to right and left.
Back: Neck firm, body forward bending.

Heart and Lungs: Hopping on right and left, and on both feet.
Quieting: Calf work.
Breathing: Arm swinging out.

Lesson No. 4.

Order Exercises: Hips firm. Stride toe stand. Hands clasped on head.
Leg: Front leg work, raise toes.
Head: Hand on head, head to right and left bend.
Arms: Twist entire arm, in four positions.
Balancing: Stand on one foot.
Shoulders: The position of a diver.
Thorax: Arm swinging front and up.
Waist: Hips firm. Turn body to right and left.
Back: Feet close, hips firm, body forward bending.
Heart and Lungs: Running in place.
Quieting: Front leg work.
Breathing: Arm swinging front.

Lesson No. 5.

Order Exercises: Letter Y, neck firm, stride toe stand.
Legs: Flex the legs (back thigh).
Head: Head to right and left turn.
Arms: Flex and extend arms.
Balancing: Stand on one foot, arms up.
Shoulders: From position of a soldier, take letter Y.
Thorax: Arm swinging up, slapping hands above head. Arm swinging front, up, back, and down.
Waist: Stride standing, backward bending, neck firm.
Back: Bending obliquely forward to right and left, hips firm.
Heart and Lungs: Hopping, separate and touch the feet.
Quieting: Flex the legs.
Breathing: Arm swinging front.

Lesson No. 6.

Order Exercises: Letter Y, feet close, toe standing.

Leg: Half lower body (front thigh).
Head: Head backward forcing.
Arms: Flex and rotate arms.
Balancing: Stand on one foot, swinging other leg forward and backward.
Shoulders: Arms front, out, and down.
Thorax: Body forward bend, arm thrusting up.
Waist: Backward bending, neck firm.
Back: Forward bending, neck firm.
Heart and Lungs: Hopping, separating and touching feet.
Quieting: Half lower body.
Breathing: Arm swinging out and up.

Lesson No. 7.

Order Exercises: The charging position.
Leg: Leg swinging for hip region.
Head: Head backward force, neck firm.
Arm: Deltoid, arm swinging.
Balancing: Stand on one foot, and point the other leg front, out, and back.
Shoulder: Elevate the right and lower the left by arm flexion and extension.
Thorax: Arm bending and extending upward.
Waist: Arms up, body bending to right and left.
Back: Forward bending, neck firm. Feet close.
Heart and Lungs: Running in place, increasing the number of times.
Quieting: Leg swinging for hip region.
Breathing: Arm swinging out and up.

Lesson No. 8.

Order Exercises: Charging position with arms up. Arm flinging position.
Leg: Thigh flexing.
Head: Rolling motions.
Arm: Position of arm flinging and elbow out.
Balancing: Place rest, and on the heels stand.

Shoulder: Setting up exercise No. 1.
Thorax: Arms front, out, up, and down.
Waist: Arms up, body bending to right and left.
Back: Forward bending, neck firm. Walk stand.
Heart and Lungs: Running in place, increasing the number of times.
Quieting: Thigh flexing.
Breathing: Arm swinging front and up.

Lesson No. 9.

Order Exercises: Arms out, and body turn to right and left.
Leg: Raise on toes, then half lower body.
Head: Head backward bending, with resistance.
Arm: Flex arm, extend arm, and deltoid work.
Balancing: Both mark time and halt on heels.
Shoulder: Setting up exercise No. 2.
Thorax: Charging position, arm thrusting up.
Waist: Body bending backward, arms up.
Back: Forward bending, arms up.
Heart and Lungs; Running in place, increasing the number of times.
Quieting: Raise on toes and half lower body.
Breathing: Arm swinging front and up.

DUMB BELLS.

Below will be found a division of dumb bell work for use at each lesson. The drills themselves are somewhat old, but are given more to illustrate the methods of dividing lessons than to call attention to the drills themselves. The author recommends the Roberts bell drill for young men (R. J. Roberts, Y. M. C. A., Boston, Mass.), also the Hitchcock dumb bell drill used at Amherst College (Dr. Edward Hitchcock, Amherst, Mass).

The book entitled "Light Gymnastics" has not been revised by the author and is not therefore up to date in all respects, but it will be of assistance to the beginner.

Young teachers should be original if possible and not depend too much on others.

The pages mentioned refer to "Light Gymnastics."

Lessons Nos. 1 to 5. The alphabet.

(1) Attention.
  Bells on hips.
  Bells on chest, *a b.*
  Bells on shoulders, *a b.* Page 117.
(2) Salutes.
  Bells at back.
  Arms folded.
  Bells under shoulders.
(3) Angles.
  Circling motions.
(4) Flexing.
  Swinging.
  Twisting.
  Striking motions.
(5) Anvil strike.
  Pushing the bell.

Lessons Nos. 6 and 7. First series.

(6) Nos. I., II., III., IV., V., VI.
(7) Nos. VII., VIII., IX., X., XI., XII. Page 123.

Lessons Nos. 8, 9, and 10. Second series.

(8) Nos. I., II., V.
(9) Nos. III., IV., VII.
(10) Nos. VI. and VII. Page 125.

Lessons Nos. 11 and 12. The arm.

(11) Develop forearm.
(12) Develop upper arm.

Lessons Nos. 13 and 14. Marching series.
(13) Nos. I., II., III.
(14) Nos. IV., V. Page 130.

Lessons Nos. 15 and 16. Marching series.
(15) Circling motions.
(16) Thrusting motions. Page 130.

Lessons Nos. 17 to 21. Third series.
(17) Nos. I., II., III.
(18) Nos. IV., V., VI., VIII.
(19) Nos. IX., X., XI.
(20) Nos. XII., XIII.
(21) Nos. XIV., XV. Page 126.

Lessons Nos. 22 and 23. Third marching series.
(22) Nos. I., II., III., V., VI.
(23) Nos. VII., VIII., X., XI., XII. Page 130.

Lessons Nos. 24 to 27. Anvil Chorus.
(24) Nos. I., II., VI.
(25) Nos. III., IV., VII., VIII.
(26) Nos. V., IX., X.
(27) Nos. XI., XII. Page 131.

Lessons Nos. 28 to 30. The thorax.
(28) Widen the chest.
(29) Deepen the chest.
(30) Breathing exercises.

Lessons Nos. 31 to 33. Pizzicati Chorus.
(31) Nos. I., II., V.
(32) Nos. III., IV., VI.
(33) Nos. VII., VIII., IX., X., XI. Page 134.

THE WANDS.

Much that has been said about the bells will apply to the wands. There is such a variety of motions with this piece of apparatus that we can only call attention to some of the exercises.

Lessons Nos. 1 to 3. The alphabet.

(1) Nos. I., II., III., IV., V.
(2) Nos. VI., VII., VIII., IX.
(3) Nos. X., XI., XII.   Page 83.

Lessons Nos. 4 to 6. Marching series.

(4) Nos. I., II., III., IV., V.
(5) Nos. VI., VII., VIII.
(6) The entire alphabet.   Page 89.

Lessons Nos. 7 and 8. First series.

(7) Take Nos. I. to VIII.
(8) Take the rest of the lesson.   Page 89.

Lessons Nos. 9 to 12. Second series.

(9) Nos. I., II., III.
(10) Nos. IV., V., VI.
(11) Nos. VII., VIII., IX.
(12) No. X.   Page 91.

Lessons Nos. 13 to 21. Third series.

(13) Nos. I., II., III.
(14) Nos. IV., V., VI.
(15) Nos. VII., VIII., IX.
(16, 17) The winding motions.
(18) No. X.
(19) No. XI.
(20) No. XII.
(21) No. XIII.   Page 96.

Lessons Nos. 22 to 24. Manual of arms.

(22) Present, Charge, Port.
(23) Order, Parade rest, Carry arms.
(24) Inspect and fire.   Page 103.

Lessons Nos. 25 and 26. Bayonet drill.
(25) Right and left guard, Parries and high guard.
(26) Thrust to rear, high, middle, and low. Page 108.

Club Swinging.

The following arrangement of movements in club swinging, which comprise thirty lessons, does not cover the ground. One who has handled clubs for several years will find that there is yet much to learn. Page 139.

Lesson No. 1.—Position. "Pass." Heart-shaped circles out. Pendulum (single club).
Lesson No. 2.—Heart-shaped circles reversed.
Lesson No. 3.—Heart-shaped circles to the front.
Lesson No. 4.—Heart-shaped circles to the rear.
Lesson No. 5.—Double heart-shaped circles to the right and left and out.
Lesson No. 6—Double pendulum and lower front circle.
Lesson No. 7.—Shoulder circles reversed.
Lessons Nos. 8 and 9.—Shoulder circles front.
Lessons Nos. 10 and 11.—Shoulder circles out.
Lesson No. 12.—Halves of complete circles reversed.
Lesson No. 13.—Halves of complete circles out.
Lessons Nos. 14 and 15.—Complete shoulder circles out.
Lessons Nos. 16 and 17.—Complete circles reversed.
Lesson No. 18.—Heart-shaped circles follow time.
Lesson No. 19.—Same circles reel time.
Lesson No. 20.—The drop outside.
Lesson No. 21.—The drop inside.
Lesson No. 22.—The raise outside.
Lesson No. 23.—The raise inside.
Lesson No. 24.—The single overhead parallel.
Lesson No. 25.—The reel.
Lesson No. 26.—The follow.
Lessons Nos. 27, 28, and 29.—Single lower back.
Lesson No. 30.—The double lower back.

Lessons 1, 2, 3, and 4 are taken with one club.

School Fencing.

Method of arranging the lessons in broadsword fencing for school use:

Lessons Nos. 1 and 2.—Half face. Feet at 90 degrees. Bend knees. Advance foot and place arms in position. (Use no sword.)

Lesson No 3.—On guard, advance and retreat by steps. (No sword.)

Lesson No. 4.—On guard, advance and retreat by leaps. (No sword.)

Lesson No. 5.—On guard, using the sword for the first time.

Lesson No. 6.—Head, cheek, and shoulder guard.

Lesson No. 7.—Leg guards.

Lesson No. 8.—Practice all guards. Advance, retreat, and sway.

Lesson No. 9.—Form twos and give head blow.

Lesson No. 10.—Cheek and shoulder blows.

Lesson No. 11.—Leg blows.

Lesson No. 12.—Practice all blows.

Lesson No. 13.—Lunging.

Lesson No. 14.—Lunging and striking.

Lesson No. 15.—Begin the series.

For details see page 171.

DIVISION OF WORK IN A JUNIOR CLASS FOR ONE YEAR.

Yearly division of light gymnastics in the junior class of the Anderson Normal School of Gymnastics.

Subject.	September and October.	November.	December.	January.	February.	March.	April.
Free Work.	Alphabet. Order exercise. Leg exercise. Neck exercise.	Alphabet. Arms.	Personal work. Balancing exercises.	Personal work. Shoulders.	Thorax. Heart and lungs.	Attitudes. Waist and back.	School work.
Dancing: Stage, Society, Walking.	Society dancing.	Society dancing.	Minuet.	Stage dancing.	Stage dancing.	Stage dancing.	Stage dancing.
Fancy Steps.	Primary exercises.	Primary motions.	Primary motions.	Secondary motions.	Fancy steps.	Fancy steps.	Fancy steps.
Emerson System.					Emerson system.	Emerson system.	Emerson system.
Military Evolutions.	Military work.	Military work.	Military work.	Military work.	Military work.	Military work.	Military work.
Fancy Marching.		Fancy marching.	Fancy marching.	Fancy marching.	Stage marching.	Stage marching.	Stage marching.
Dumb Bell Drills.	Alphabet. Developing exercises.	Series 1 and 2. Anvil Chorus. Arm exercise.	Series 2. Anvil Chorus. Balancing.	Series 3. Marching. Shoulder ex. Pizzicati.	Series 3. Attitudes. Thorax ex. Pizzicati.	Rataplan. Back exercise. Waist.	Series 2. Series 3. German drill.
Club Swinging.	Alphabet.	Long circles. Series 1.	Short circles. Series 1.	Combinations. Series 1.	Snakes. Series 2.	Snakes. Series 2.	Series 2. Series 3.
Wand Drill.	Alphabet.	Alphabet. Arm exercise.	Series 2. Balancing exercise.	Series 2. Shoulder exercise. Marching.	Series 3. Thorax ex. Manual of arms.	Series 3. Waist and back ex. Marching. Manual of arms.	Series 3. Marching. Postures. Bayonet drill.
Pole Drill. Combination Work.			Single poles.	Single poles. Bells and wands.	Double poles. Bells and wands.	Double poles. Wands and poles.	Bells, wands, and poles.
Hoop Drill.			Group 1.	Group 2.	Group 3.	Group 4.	Group 5.

A LIST OF BOOKS FOR REFERENCE.

Arnaud and Delausmone : *The Delsarte System*.
Ascham : *Schoolmaster*.
Baine : *Education as a Science*.
Baine : *Lectures on the Science and Art of Education*.
Bishop : *Americanized Delsarte Culture*.
Browning : *Educational Theories*.
Comenius : *Great Didactic*.
Compayre : *History of Pedagogy*.
Compayre : *Lectures on Pedagogy*.
Everett : *Primer of Ethics*.
Fitch : *Lectures on Teaching*.
Hall : *Pedagogical Seminary*.
Hughes : *Mistakes in Teaching*.
Johonnot : *Practice of Teaching*.
Kirke : *Hand-book of Physiology*.
Locke : *Thoughts Concerning Education*.
Milton : *Tractate on Education*.
Oscar Browning : *Practice of Education*.
Parker : *Talks on Teaching*.
Payne : *Theory, Practice, and History of Education*.
Pestalozzi : *Leonard and Gertrude*.
Posse : *Kinesiology*.
Preyer : *Infant Mind*.
Quick : *Lives of Educational Reformers*.
Rousseau : *Emile*.
Seaver : *Physical Diagnosis*.
Spencer : *Education*.
Sweet : *Methods of Teaching*.
Thring : *Theory and Practice of Teaching*.
White : *School Management*.

INDEX.

Alignments, 201.
Alphabet, 158.
American system, 47.
Amiel, 54.
Analysis, 111.
Anderson, H. S., 13.
Ankle, 123.
Anvil Chorus, 223.
Aristotle, 32, 56.
Arms, 124.
Arnold, 25.
Attention, 84, 183.
Automatic movements, 113.
Back, 64.
Back step, 198.
Bain, 19.
Balancing movements, 63.
Base, common, 15; narrow, 15; wide, 15.
Basedow, 22, 83, 105.
Bells, 216.
Bishop, 47.
Blackston, 19.
Blaikie, 79.
Bolin, 12, 68.
Bowne, B. P., 49.
Boys, how to teach, 171.
Breal, 93.
Breathing, 135, 145.
Brosius, 186.
Browning, 33, 77.
Buisson, 104.
Carlyle, 22, 54.
Change step, 196.
Changing weight, 155.
Charging motion, 159.
Charge, reverse, 160.
Chauvet, 28.
Chest, 134.
Chivalry, 34.
Circling motions, 161.
Clark, 38, 55.
Club swinging, 261.
Clubs, 229.
Comenius, 22, 164.
Commands, 164.
Compayre, 26.
Condillac, 84.
Corporal punishment, 100, 105.
Cowper, 54.
Day's order, 57.
Defects, 149.
Delsarte, 40, 46.
Deltoid, 128.
Denzel, 28.
De Quincey, 54.
De Saussure, 28, 86, 91.
Developing work, 14.
Dickinson, Dr. R. L., 20, 38, 146.
Directions, 150.
Discipline, 95.
Division of work for year, 245.
Double time, 200.
Drop circle, 235.
Dumb bells, 216, 257.
Education, general, 26.
Eggleston, Edward, 102.
Eliot, 76.
Emerson, R. W., 38, 55.
Enebuske, 69.
Ethics, 40.
Exercise, compound, 14; double, 14; simple, 14.
Exercises, primary, 14; secondary, 14.
Facings, right and left, 190.
Fencing, 238, 262.
Fitz, 70.
Flank movements, 208.
Foot extension and flexion, 155.
Foot raising, 155.
Football, 50.
Form fours from a line, 211.
Form fours from file of twos, 208.
Form twos from fours, 210.
Form twos from a line, 210.
Form twos and fours from file, 208.
Fours right or left, 211.
French program, 38.
Froebel, 22, 23, 24, 38, 39.
Gargantua, 37.
German system, 45, 46.
Government, 95.
Grace, 45, 117.
Grant, Horace, 86.
Greeks, 29, 31.
Gulick, Dr. Luther, 238.
Guts Muth, 45.
Gymnastic selection, 58; totality, 58; unity, 59.
Gymnastics, æsthetic, 14; corrective, 14; educational, 13; free, 14, 248; heavy, 14; light, 14; medical, 13; military, 14, 183, 245.

Hall, G. Stanley, 55, 76, 111.
Halt, 194.
Hartwell, Dr. E. M., 41.
Head, 122.
Health, 115.
Heave-movements, 62.
Hitchcock, Dr. E., 92, 257.
Hopping, 162.
Hour division, 178.
Hughes, 20.
Huxley, 37.
Interest, 83.
Introductory movements, 61.
Ireson, Jennie M., 90.
Jacotot, 22, 25.
James, 53.
Joly, 28.
Kant, 27, 94, 105.
Kellogg, Dr., 146.
Kingsley, 56.
Knee bending, 154.
Kyphosis, 147.
Ladd, 70.
La Grange, 146.
Leg movements, 61, 65, 66.
Leg swinging, 155.
Legs, 123.
Le Row, C. B., 100.
Letter "Y", 139.
Ling, 12, 13, 68.
Locke, 22, 35, 83, 105.
Lunging motions, 162.
Luther, 34.
Mahaffy, 29.
Mann, 56.
Mannerisms, 242.
March, by the flank, 203; in file, 189; in line, 202; to the rear, 191.
Marion, 28, 56.
Marking time, 192.
Mays, Dr., 146.
Melancthon, 35.
Memory exercises, 119.
Military gymnastics, 14, 183, 245.
Mill, 20, 22, 28.
Milton, 37.
Mistakes in teaching, 106.
Montaigne, 35, 106.
Morrill, A. B., 221.
Mosher, Dr. E. M., 163, 188.
Munger, 54.
Music, 35.
Neck, 122.
Niemeyer, 28.
Opinions of educators, 16.
Oblique face, 189.
Oblique march, 205.
Order movements, 60.
Order of exercises, 12.
Parker, 55, 99.
Pascal, 54.
Payne, 24, 25, 26, 27, 30, 86, 91.

Pedagogy, 26.
Pestalozzi, 22, 26.
Philbrick, John, 22.
Physical education, German, 40; Greek, 29; opinions on, 29; Roman, 32; Swedish, 40.
Physique, 116.
Place rest, 188.
Placing, 161.
Platform, 9.
Plato, 27, 32, 171.
Play, 24, 39.
Posse, Baron, 68, 139, 185.
Precipitant movements, 66.
Pulse-rate, 68.
Quarter circle, 142.
Quick, 36.
Rabelais, 26, 37, 105.
Ratich, 22, 23.
Reel, 235.
Reflex acts, 111.
Reformers, 34.
Relations of teacher to parent, 109.
Respiratory exercises, 66.
Reverse charge, 160.
Richards, E. L., 83, 118.
Richter, Jean Paul, 102.
Right, forward, fours right, 212.
Roberts, R. J., 138, 167.
Round work, 120.
Rousseau, 22, 28, 36.
Running, 163.
Sarcasm, 100.
Schmidt, 46.
School government, 95.
Scripture, 70.
Seaver, 70, 145, 230.
Seldon, 18.
Self-control, 117.
Self-reliance, 117.
Shoulders, 130.
Side movements, 65.
Simon, 28.
Skarstrom, 43.
Snake, 236.
Socrates, 29, 32.
Spencer, 18, 22, 28, 29, 39, 87, 97.
Spine, 147.
Starting, 193.
Step, back, 198; long, 199; short, 199; side, 198.
Stepping motion, 158.
Stimulus, 76.
Strength, 115.
Sully, 93.
Swaying, 153, 161.
Swedish day's order, 12.
Swedish system, 12, 45, 74.
Swett, 38, 104.
Swinging motions, 161.
Synthesis, 111.

INDEX. 269

Tense-bendings, 61.
Terms, 13.
Thigh swinging, 156.
Thorax, 134.
Trotzendorf, 35.
Twos, right or left, 210, 211.
Tyndall, 21.
Voice, 164.

Walking, how to teach, 151.
Wands, 226, 259.
Warner, 46.
Wheelings, 205.
Who should teach? 115.
Why do we teach? 115.
Will, 118.
Xenophon, 29.

www.ingramcontent.com/pod-product-compliance
Lightning Source LLC
Chambersburg PA
CBHW032117230426
43672CB00009B/1764